VISIONS AND REVISIONS
of American Poetry

VISIONS
AND
REVISIONS

of American Poetry

by Lewis Putnam Turco

The University of Arkansas Press
Fayetteville   1986

LIBRARY OF CONGRESS CATALOGING IN PUBLICATION DATA

Turco, Lewis Putnam.
  Visions and revisions.

Includes index.
  1. American poetry—History and criticism—Addresses,
essays, lectures. I. Title.
PS305.T87 1986   811'.009   85-1056
ISBN 0-938626-49-3
ISBN 0-938626-50-7 (pbk.)

For May Putnam Turco, 1899–1985,
who complained that I never use my middle name,
in loving recollection.

Books by Lewis Turco

The Book of Forms: A Handbook of Poetics (1968)
The Literature of New York: A Bibliography (1970)
Poetry: An Introduction through Writing (1973)

Poetry Collections

First Poems (1960)
Awaken, Bells Falling: Poems 1959–1967 (1968)
The Inhabitant (1970)
Pocoangelini: A Fantography & Other Poems (1971)
Seasons of the Blood (1980)
American Still Lifes (1981)
The Compleat Melancholick (1985)

Acknowledgments

The essays in this book have been considerably reworked, for the most part, from the versions that appeared as reviews and articles in the following periodicals:

Midwest Review, Spring 1961; *The Mad River Review*, Spring-Summer 1965; *Arts in Society*, iii: 2, 1965; *Michigan Quarterly Review*, January 1968, Winter 1975, and Spring 1977; *American Weave*, June 1968; *Concerning Poetry*, Fall 1968 and Spring 1973; *Carleton Miscellany*, Winter 1969 and Summer 1980; *New England Review*, July-August 1969; *Poetry*, August 1971; *Modern Poetry Studies*, iii: 2, 1972; *English Record*, Spring 1973 and Summer 1974; *Costerus: Essays in English and American Language and Literature* (Amsterdam), Vol. viii, 1973; *Poetry Pilot*, November 1973; *Andover Review*, Fall 1974; *Contemporary Poetry: A Journal of Criticism*, iv: 3, 1982; *Escarpments*, Autumn 1983.

"The Matriarchy of American Poetry" was first published in *College English* 34:8 (May 1973). Copyright 1973 by the National Council of Teachers of English, by whose permission the essay is reprinted.

"Sympathetic Magic" is reprinted from *American Poets in 1976*, edited by William Heyen (Indianapolis: Bobbs-Merrill, 1976).

"*The Waste Land* Revisited" was first published (as "*The Waste Land* Reconsidered") in the *Sewanee Review* 87 (April 1979). Copyright 1979 by Lewis Turco.

Poem credits are as follows: *Ontario Review* for "Poetry," edited from lines in Emily Dickinson's letters; "A Dedication," from *Awaken, Bells Falling*, University of Missouri Press, copyright 1968; "Lorrie," from *Pocoangelini: A Fantography and Other Poems*, Despa Press, copyright 1962 and 1971; "Mary Moody Emerson, R.I.P.," "Tick" and "The Dream," from *The Weed Garden*, Peaceweed Press, copyright 1973; "Fetch," from *A Cage of Creatures*, The Banjo Press, copyright 1978; and "The Moon of Melancholy," from *The Compleat Melancholick*, The Bieler Press, copyright 1985 by Lewis Turco, all rights reserved.

"Professional Poet," by Robert Francis, is reprinted from *The Satirical Rogue on Poetry*, by Robert Francis (Amherst: University of Massachusetts Press, 1968). Copyright © 1968 by Robert Francis.

Passages from James Dickey, *Babel to Byzantium* (New York, 1968), are reprinted by permission of Farrar, Straus & Giroux, Inc.

Passages from Alfred Kreymborg, *Our Singing Strength* (New York: Coward McCann, 1929), are reprinted by permission of The Putnam Publishing Group.

Passages from Hyatt H. Waggoner, *American Poets from the Puritans to the Present*, Revised Edition (Baton Rouge, 1984), are reprinted by permission of Louisiana State University Press and Hyatt H. Waggoner. Copyright © 1968, 1984, by Hyatt H. Waggoner.

Acknowledgment and thanks also to the corporation of Yaddo for two residencies; the Research Foundation of the State University of New York for several fellowships since 1966, and the SUNY College at Oswego for two sabbatical leaves. During all of these, work was done on various portions of this book of criticism.

Contents

VISIONS AND REVISIONS
of American Poetry

Introduction

How does one come to poetry?
In my case, accidentally and inevitably, perhaps even genetically. Begin with heritage: my middle name is *Putnam*, which is my mother's maiden name. She was a determined young woman who, in a day when it was not a likely thing to do, lifted herself by the bootstraps off a rundown Wisconsin farm and turned herself into a Methodist missionary by working her way through Boston University. She is a direct descendant of Constable "Carolina" John Putnam, who, in 1692, was rounding up the innocent citizens of Salem Village and dragging them off to jail to await trial for witchcraft.

According to the family genealogy, *The Putnam Lineage* by Eben Putnam (Salem, 1907), George Puttenham, author of *The Arte of English Poesy* (1589), was a member of the clan in a line that became extinct. Perhaps the genes survived, however, for in 1968 I published, after eight years of research and before I owned a copy of cousin Eben's book, *The Book of Forms: A Handbook of Poetics*.

Go to inevitability next: I grew up in a house that was full of books, and I began reading them early. Along the way I began to write because I wanted to do for people what other authors had done for me. They had made life bearable, even enjoyable on those occasions when the magic of the written word opened doors into the landscape of the mind. In the third grade I would tell my friends Jackie Tierney and Curt Offen episodes of a serial adventure made up as we walked the mile to—strangely, now that I think of it—the Israel Putnam School on Broad Street in Meriden, Connecticut. In later years I would sit in my father's study, bent over the keyboard of his elderly standard typewriter, and peck out poems and stories one key at a time—that is, I would do so when he wasn't using the typewriter himself to write—painfully and painstakingly—the English language sermons he would deliver on Sunday in the First Italian Baptist Church, of which he was pastor.

My first published story won a prize and appeared in a local paper, the *Morning Record*, in 1949, when I was fifteen years old; not long thereafter, my poems began to appear regularly in the same daily in Lydia Atkinson's column, "Pennons of Pegasus." Dudley Fitts told me at Bread Loaf in 1961 that ten years earlier, when he used to teach in a prep school one town over, he would read "Pennons" every Wednesday to his wife, and they would spend fifteen minutes or so howling with laughter. I had already begun entertaining people, one of them a famous classical scholar, no less.

Go next to the accidental. In 1952 I enlisted in the U.S. Navy straight out of Meriden High School, and I served four years—two of them at sea aboard the *Hornet*, a carrier—as a yeoman, which means "clerk." The Navy taught me to type and gave me plenty of leisure—there is little for a yeoman to do while at sea. I spent the time reading, writing, and *learning* to write: I had sent a bad poem to a magazine, and the editor had rejected it. She'd told me I ought to read the "moderns" and do the exercises in Mary J. J.

Wrinn's high school poetry writing textbook *The Hollow Reed* (1935). (Wrinn was, incidentally, Delmore Schwartz's high school teacher, and she had included some of his early work among the student poems in her anthology.) Perhaps, if I did these things, in ten years or so I would become a poet.

This pronouncement infuriated me, so I did as that editor suggested, and a few months later I submitted some more poems to her. She took two of them, though she admonished me to "watch those word flings!" and they were published in 1953 when I was nineteen years of age. By the time I got to the University of Connecticut in 1956 my work had appeared in some reputable places— *Antioch Review, Talisman, New Orleans Poetry Journal,* and Harold Vinal's *Voices*—Vinal was the editor e. e. cummings shredded in his poem "Beauty Hurts Mr. Vinal."

Perhaps the reader will have noticed that I had taught myself to write systematically. Further, I was evidently a "natural" formalist, though I wasn't aware of it at the time. I wasn't a rigid traditionalist, however, for I loved experimental writing also (including cummings). In fact, my tastes were eclectic. I didn't, and I still don't, care what sort of thing anyone writes, so long as it is well done. My own work has been both praised and condemned for the wide range of formal approaches that I employ. The one thing I didn't care for was sloppy writing, and in 1959, when Mr. Vinal asked me, while I was still an undergraduate, to do some reviewing, I had to sit down and think about what it was I did, and what I liked and disliked in others' work.

In my second review for *Voices,* "The Poet's Court" (No. 171, 1960), I set forth my criteria for judging a poem. They were simple. I conceived of a poem as operating on several levels simultaneously: the typographical (shaped, stanzaic, strophic; regular or irregular line lengths), the sonic (rhymes, meters, alliterations, consonances, other effects of language music); the sensory (the evocation of the five senses and of emotion); the ideational (subject, meaning, theme), and the fusional—whether and how the other levels dovetail, merge, and support one another.

Having done my duty by explaining my position as a critic, I continued to use my "levels of poetry" in my own writing, both creative and critical, but I made no more of them publicly until one day, while visiting a writers' conference, I heard Loring Williams—Hart Crane's uncle by marriage and the editor of a small press and magazine in Cleveland—use the system of levels in his workshop. His students seemed to understand his remarks about their poems, given this uncomplicated frame of reference. From then on I, too, used the levels in my classes and, eventually, in *The Book of Forms*.

Two things happened in 1968, the year of my handbook's publication, that caused my literary world to quake and sunder. First, I was told by a mutual friend that a teaching poet had exclaimed, on hearing of the appearance of *The Book of Forms*, "Oh, [crap]! Now I've got to learn all that stuff" (though in fact he never did). I had long been going on the assumption that everyone was interested in the craft of writing, especially teachers and critics. If I was bone-numbingly naive, it must be remembered that, though I had eventually attended college and graduate school, I was largely an autodidact in poetry and poetics, and that I had found subsequently, both at Connecticut and at Iowa, teachers who reinforced my illusions, who really *were* interested in such things, teachers whom I respected and admired: Norman Friedman and John Malcolm Brinnin at UConn, Paul Engle and Donald Justice at Iowa. Friedman was an Aristotelian critic, a cummings scholar, and a poet not much older than I; Brinnin, the finest practical critic I have ever run across; Paul Engle, an empirical idealist, if that is not an oxymoron; and Justice, a brilliant teacher and a fine writer with an interest in theoretics. It was he who encouraged me to begin work on *The Book of Forms* when, incredibly enough, I discovered that no one in English literature, not even George Puttenham, had done so obvious a thing as to gather together all the forms used traditionally in poetry and lay them out in schematic diagrams so that anyone could understand their architecture.

The other thing that happened in 1968 was that Hyatt H. Waggoner published his book *American Poets from the Puritans to the Present*. This treatise happened to appear at a time when I was confused about a good many things, including the situation of American poetry as I had always perceived it and the way things were in actuality. Waggoner's book cleared up many of my mazlements. It made me see much about poetry starkly for the first time, and it helped me to understand myself better, myself and some of the things I had been groping toward as a poet. It also showed me what many other poets had been trying to do, and I saw that all of us were grappling with similar problems in this century and civilization.

What was Waggoner's central thesis? Briefly, that Ralph Waldo Emerson is the polar figure in American poetry. It is he who represents the viewpoint that differentiates "American" from "British" poetry. "Mainstream" American poetry is visionary, whereas in the Old World the poet was more prone to see himself as the maker, the artificer of language. Emerson, in his essay "The Poet," put it this way:

The signs and credentials of the poet are, that he announces that which no man foretold. He is the true and only doctor; he knows and tells; he is the only teller of news, for he was present and privy to the appearance which he describes. He is a beholder of ideas, and an utterer of the necessary and causal. For we do not speak now of men of poetical talents, or of industry and skill in metre, but of the true poet.

The poet of America, then, is no kind of literary person. He or she is "the sayer, the namer." Poetry, to Emerson and Emersonian poets such as Whitman and Crane, is not any kind of performance or entertainment, it is a revelation of the "truth" transcendentally perceived.

For it is not metres, but a metre-making argument, that makes a poem—a thought so passionate and alive, that, like the spirit of a plant or an animal, it has an architecture of its own, and adorns nature with a new thing. The thought and the form are equal in the order of time, but in the order of genesis the thought is prior to form. The poet has a new thought: he has a whole new experience to unfold; he will tell us how it was with him, and all men will be the richer in his fortune. For the experience of each new age requires a new confession, and the world seems always waiting for its poet.

I am not convinced that Emerson is right, but I *am* persuaded that many American poets think and have thought so, even when they have not read Emerson specifically, but only been inhabited unconsciously by his pervasive spirit.

Two things emerged from the book. First, the reader saw in perspective the warring in America between Makers (to use the old Scottish term for bards—*makirs*) and Sayers as each viewpoint attempted to dominate the literary scene. Second, one saw, as in Emerson himself, that most major American poetry, especially in the twentieth century, is part of an immense religious and philosophical debate—among mechanists, humanists, various kinds of romantics, existentialists, hedonists, evangelists, traditional religionists—which continues into the present.

At that point I began a friendship and a correspondence with Dr. Waggoner which continues to this day, and I began to write essays on American poetry myself, essays which continued these religious and literary debates. On occasion I even wrote a poem that embodied one or the other or both viewpoints, and I would enclose a copy in my letters now and again, as for instance this one:

Mary Moody Emerson, R.I.P.
(*for Hyatt H. Waggoner*)

Ralph Waldo's Aunt Mary,
moody as all getout, got herself
rigged out in a shroud and rode
through Concord on a donkey
"to get herself in the habit of the

tomb." Ralph Waldo, though she
wore her cerements daily ever
after, reckoned her beast of
burden was more symbolic
than her garb. If he could transcend Calvin
concordantly, why not
she? Ceremonies of innocence
and hope lay everywhere be-
fore her grave step, were she but
to look: "There grow the Leaves of Grass." *But what*
makes them so green? "On the
village square a concourse of elms praises
the good Lord." *In their shadow*
the moss grows. "All are Elect!"
Then why so few who can see? Ralph Waldo
shrugged and put down to whim this
relative moodiness. When they put
her down at last in her life-
long weeds, Ralph Waldo blessed her
blind eyes as, no doubt, Aunt Mary blessed his.

LEWIS PUTNAM TURCO
Oswego, New York
20 May 1985

The Pro-Am Tournament

Alfred Kreymborg says in his neglected history of American poetry, *Our Singing Strength*, that Anne Bradstreet "remains the first of Americans to choose a poetic career." She was our first professional poet. According to Hyatt H. Waggoner, in *American Poets*, Edward Taylor was our first amateur and our first "Emersonian."

Mrs. Bradstreet's *The Tenth Muse, Lately Sprung Up in America* was published, significantly, in England, not in America, in 1650. Kreymborg writes: "She is by no means The Tenth Muse she was christened; nor is her style, copied after her ponderous English master, Joshua Sylvester, worthy of more than sympathy. But she left appealing memories of the gentler aspects of Puritan life in the reveries of a Puritan wife and mother."

Waggoner agrees, more or less, noting that "very little of the verse in her first volume . . . seems today to justify the title. . . ."

But 'Contemplations,' which was published only after her death in the revised and augmented collection that appeared in 1687, shows her growing self-confidence and skill. 'Contemplations' could be called our first nature poem, though *she* would not have thought of it that way. When she contemplates the splendor of a New England autumn, with its colors that seem 'painted' but are really 'true,' she finds her senses 'rapt' and hardly knows what she ought to feel,

> I wist not what to wish, yet sure, thought I,
> If so much excellence abide below
> How excellent is He that dwells on high,
> Whose power and beauty by his works we know.
>
> (*American Poets*, p. 8)

"If this foreshadows Bryant," Waggoner goes on, perhaps with a sense of disappointment in not discovering more vatic or Platonic spirit behind this Puritan matter, "other parts of the poem introduce themes and images that have continued to engage our poets through several centuries." Not only themes and images— constructions and a way of seeing as well, not to mention a tradition of gentility that continues to haunt the schoolroom and the American consciousness when it regards the subject of poetry.

Bradstreet's earliest pieces, those in the 1650 edition, were largely technical exercises. She imitated English masters and used English meters; she tried to reproduce England, her native country, not New England. It was, perhaps, a way of keeping interested in life, in staying alive intellectually in a rigorous spiritual and physical climate. Keeping the mind alert has never been easy for a woman in American society; what must it have been like in Puritan Boston? Fortunately, Anne Bradstreet was the wife of a governor, and she had indulgences not accorded many others of her sex. If her early pieces, however, were all we had to remember of her, we would not remember.

Anne Bradstreet did not set out to be America's first professional poet. She had the distinction thrust upon her by well-meaning relatives and friends who took it into their own condescending male hands to pamper this harmless vanity of composition. What hurt could it do? "But," as Adrienne Rich points out, "she was a spirited woman with a strong grasp on reality; and temperament,

experience, and the fact of having reached a wider audience con-
verged at this point to give Anne Bradstreet a new assurance."

Her poems were being read seriously by strangers, though not in the form
she would have chosen to send them out. Her intellectual delight was no
longer vulnerable to carping ('Theyl say my hand a needle better fits'); it
was a symptom neither of vanity nor infirmity; she had carried on her
woman's life conscientiously while composing her book. It is probable
that some tension of self-distrust was relaxed, some inner vocation con-
firmed, by the publication and praise of *The Tenth Muse*. But the word
'vocation' must be read in a special sense. Not once in her prose memoir
does she allude to her poems, or to the publication of her book; her story,
written out for her children, is the familiar Puritan drama of temptation
by Satan and correction by God. She would not have defined herself, even
by aspiration, as an artist. But she had crossed the line between the ama-
teur and the artist, where private dissatisfaction begins and public ap-
proval, though gratifying, is no longer of the essence. For the poet of her
time and place, poetry might be merely a means to a greater end; but the
spirit in which she wrote was not that of a dilettante. (Rich, Foreword to
The Works of Anne Bradstreet, ed. Jeannine Henley.)

Anne Bradstreet became, at this point, our first *confessional* as
well as our first *professional* poet. She was, at least in her later
poems, an egopoet, not a dramatic one, nor even a "maker," and
another American precedent was set, one that would be broken by
Emily Dickinson and Marianne Moore, but that would be ob-
served by many other women and not a few men, including Ed-
ward Taylor.

Given the United States' national bias against the profession of
letters, one felt more at ease with our first amateur poet, Edward
Taylor. Here, America was no longer in artistic competition with
England and her great makers. One might lower one's sights and
see that American poetry is all about something other than world-
view, craft, and words—it is about vision, soul, and salvation. It is
not concerned with communication on any mundane, humane
level. There must be no misunderstanding on this point. Taylor
was not any kind of great poet. Rather, his importance lay in his

foreshadowing Emerson. As Waggoner put it, "Taylor's anticipa-
tions of what was destined to become the main tradition in Ameri-
can poetry—insofar as American poetry is not simply a rather in-
ferior branch of British poetry—are somewhat more apparent in
the way he uses language and his attitude toward poetic forms
than they are in the substance of his poems."

Taylor used words "roughly." He used them for pragmatic Pu-
ritan purposes: poems were "preparatory meditations," aids in
achieving the frame of mind in which he composed his real work,
his sermons. Sometimes, of course, his poems also took the place
of the Catholic confessional. God would hear if no one else did.
Taylor would never publish his poems, not even accidentally, until
long after his death; not until the twentieth century would they
appear in print. Although he was a remarkable preacher, his status
as an amateur poet remains indisputable. We must wait for Emer-
son, who, unfortunately, was not a great poet either—he was a
great "agonist," a theoretician of poetry and its role in American
culture.

It was Emerson who laid down the ground rules for the first
"great" American poet, perhaps the *only* great American poet, ac-
cording to some: Walt Whitman. The Good Gray Poet, as he was
called, was great not necessarily because he wrote great poems,
but because he played the game according to Emerson, who in-
vented the poetic equivalent of baseball, which, to the discerning
eye, was certainly not cricket.

According to Emersonian critics, until Whitman there had been
only two currents in American poetry—imitation British, that
is, professional-artistic, and Transcendentalist, that is, amateur-
theological. If one dismisses America's professional poetry as not
even American, but something existing in Limbo somewhere over
the Atlantic above the route of the Mayflower, one is left with pure
American circa mid-nineteenth century. Unfortunately, things
soon went wrong. As Waggoner explains,

There are then not two distinct major "lines" in American poetry . . . , but three lines springing from the two figures [of Emerson and Whitman], considered separately and together. There are those poets who have responded to Emerson but not, in an important way, to Whitman. There are others, chiefly in the twentieth century, who have responded to the aspects of Whitman that are farthest from Emerson, that distinguish him from Emerson. And there are those, chiefly in the present and very recent past, who have responded to both Whitman and Emerson, or else to precisely those aspects of Whitman that are most Emersonian.

Whitman himself, and Dickinson, Robinson, and Frost are the chief of those who . . . would have written very differently, or perhaps not at all, without Emerson. They define the direct Emerson line. (*American Poets*, p. 91.)

The Whitman-minus-Emerson line was a phenomenon chiefly of the poetic renaissance of 1912 and after. In the 1920's and 1930's particularly there were poets whose Whitmanism had nothing clearly Transcendental or Emersonian about it. Carl Sandburg is perhaps the clearest example—until his latest work—but Ezra Pound is another.

The Emerson-Whitman line, broken in the later nineteenth and earlier twentieth centuries, may be traced in Hart Crane, Theodore Roethke, and a good many contemporary young poets like Denise Levertov, many of whom are not conscious of any debt to Emerson. Once or twice distilled, through Whitman and the late poems of William Carlos Williams, their kinship with Emerson is still recognizable if unavowed. (*American Poets*, pp. 91–92.)

Alas! poor Taylor, what he hath sown! There is only one element missing from this neo-Platonic, "Transcendentalist" firmament: "Furor Poeticus"—Divine Madness. The true prophet cannot be merely a transcendental philosopher, nor a Man of the People. Kreymborg says that *Leaves of Grass* "was intended for the divine average and the average ignored it, as to this day they ignore it." No, the true visionary must be mad. Fortunately, there are two candidates for this vacancy in America's poetic history: Manoah

Bodman (1764–1850) and Jones Very (1813–1880), both amateurs in good standing.

If one is looking for a true original, a native innocent in American poetry, perhaps Bodman is it. He was a lawyer, not a professional writer, but he was much more interested in the state of his soul than in law, and literature seems not to have entered into his consideration at all. Moreover, Bodman lived all his life in the remote western hills of Massachusetts and does not appear to have had contact with many outsiders other than itinerant evangelists, of whom he himself evidently was one in a small way, for there is record of his having delivered orations in neighboring villages. Bodman was contemporary with both Freneau and Bryant, but there seems little evidence that he was interested in his literary peers.

If one must make literary comparisons along Emersonian lines, however, it might be pointed out that Bodman is a forgotten link between Edward Taylor and Walt Whitman in the chain of American poets that Waggoner terms Transcendentalist or Emersonian. Bodman, in fact, pre-empted Emerson in the area of visionary experience, for he actually saw things that weren't there, and he spoke with what he thought were angels and the Christian saints for a long time—even with God himself—but he had fallen prey to Salem-style delusion, for it was at last revealed to him that these Beings were not holy, but apparitions from the Pit, out to devastate his soul. It's too bad Emerson knew nothing of Bodman. The practicing vatic might have warned the theorist of Puritan traps hidden beyond the Transcendental veil.

The reclamation of early American poets has been a major scholarly preoccupation of recent years. Bodman is no less interesting than some of the others who have been disinterred. This graveyard raiding was begun in 1960 by Donald E. Stanford, who brought to light the work of Taylor, a poet unknown to his own generation as a poet, though not as a preacher. Then, in 1965,

N. Scott Momaday brought out the first complete edition of the poems of Frederick Goddard Tuckerman, a nineteenth-century poet who was also largely unknown, or at least forgotten. To these bodies of work, Nathan Lyons added Emerson's protegé Jones Very with his edition of Very's *Selected Poems*.

These three poets have certain associations with one another: like the Calvinist Taylor, Very was a preacher, a Unitarian "Quietist." Both wrote for religious reasons, Taylor as an exercise in meditation, for the poems helped him to organize his thoughts and prepare him to preach. Very, however, believed that his own poems were divinely inspired; he was, so to speak, only the medium through whom God spoke. Reading his poems, one wonders that God has so thin a voice. Very's, and therefore Emerson's, connection with Tuckerman is stronger, for Tuckerman was Very's pupil at Harvard.

Lyons wrote a readable and informative introduction to Very's poems, though one might question its organization. In Part I, titled "The Man," there is a good deal of Very's theology and a fair amount of his remarkable poetic theory, for which, no doubt, Emerson was largely responsible. In Part II, "The Poet," there is more theology and theory. When Lyons did make some comments about Very's achievement and procedures, one was not encouraged to believe the poet is worth the trouble. If one ranges over the Introduction one finds, among a few complimentary remarks, a good many assertions of this sort:

Very's stylistic canon is . . . sharply limited . . . , [his] poems are without drama; . . . though many were written in what he claims was mystical communion, they generally only state his mystical paradoxes. . . . Invariably the sonnets are metrically regular (occasionally too facile, even monotonous) and the rhyme correct. . . . Very pads frequently, often without major damage, in the usual ways.

Jones Very evidently didn't need to resolve the structural difficulties of "mystical communion" that were to plague later Emersonian vatics, for the Lord passed his messages on to Very in sonnet form. When one examines the poems one discovers that all these things Lyons said are only too true. Even the "best" of the poems aren't good enough to justify more than a page or two in some comprehensive anthology of American poetry.

One must admire Lyons' honesty, but why bring Very forth into broad daylight under the circumstances? The answer is simple: though Very isn't a good writer, he is in the Emersonian mainstream; therefore, he's an American Good Gray Poet, not a Bad Old British Bard. One is not to honor writing and art in these United States, one is to honor vision and theology. If this be the criterion, then, of what constitutes our national poetic pantheon, perhaps Manoah Bodman and Jones Very should be granted the recognition they deserve as the greatest American poets. They are the only two who believed with their souls that they had communicated with that which is beyond. Even Walt Whitman never did that.

The Matriarchy of American Poetry

America's literary ambivalence comes in shades of dark and light: the dialogue that took place in the 1960's among Black American poets was a mirror image of the traditional professional-amateur, or artist-mystic dialogue of white American poetry. Blacks even have their own counterpart of Anne Bradstreet, Mother of the White American Muse, in Phillis Wheatley, born a century after *The Tenth Muse* had "sprung up."

Mrs. Bradstreet was a native of England. Though Phillis Wheatley was born on the west coast of Africa, she was reared in the same rigorous New England climate that had brought her predecessor to bloom. For whatever reason, however, Wheatley's spiritual home was England no less than it had been Bradstreet's. The difference was only that Anne Bradstreet's models were Puritan English; Phillis Wheatley's were Augustan English. The parallels continue: Wheatley's first publication, a translation of a story by Ovid, was published at the behest and with the aid of friends, and her first full book, *Poems on Various Subjects*, appeared in England in 1773, though a pamphlet of her work was printed in Boston in 1770.

There is no doubt that Wheatley was a prodigy and a genius. If Bradstreet had been well-received by her society, it was nothing compared with the stir made by the Black woman on both sides of the Atlantic. Wheatley emulated popular Augustan poetry to the degree that her talent, great as it was, never developed beyond mere competence, and the wonder she caused lasted no longer than her novelty. In other words, condescending whites fussed over her for reasons that were racial and biographical, not artistic, and another American precedent was set: poetry is most interesting when its creator has public-relations value; poetry is not interesting in and of itself, as a product of our culture. If it were, we would still read one or two poems by Bradstreet and Wheatley, perhaps "Contemplations" by the former and "An Hymn to the Morning" by the latter.

Wheatley's work was frozen by her talent, or the praise accorded her, or the objective neo-classical ethos of her time—more likely all these things—at that point beyond which Bradstreet began to develop a truly individual poetry. In a 1969 reprint of *The Life and Works of Phillis Wheatley*, G. Herbert Renfro said that "in translations of Ovid or Horace, she was singularly proficient." She was a professional poet serving an age dedicated to public expression, not "creative writing." She never developed to the point of personal expression, at least not in the poems she allowed to be published.

One wonders what might have happened had she torn away the Negro mask, the slave mask that protected her and kept her a celebrity rather than allowing her to develop as a poet. One wonders whether Phillis Wheatley did not, in fact, write those poems she would have had to hide or destroy, or else become a martyr. The romantic age was imminent (Emerson, immanent), and in England the so-called "pre-romantics" were writing. Even in America there were Philip Freneau and Manoah Bodman just coming on. Though Bodman was the rankest of native amateurs, and those few who read him would dismiss him as a harmless crank, Freneau was not an amateur, and he wrote in two styles—neo-classical and "pre-romantic."

Did Wheatley secretly do the same? She wrote largely at night. Did she confess her darkness into shadow and destroy the confession? Useless speculation—we can probably never know. Certainly no one ever had more cause for ambivalence, for cultural dissociation, than a lone Black female living as a slave in a patrician house in Boston. One hint only—Renfro quotes "one who had every opportunity for knowing" to the effect that " 'she did not seem to have the power of retaining the creations of her own fancy for a long time in her mind. If during the vigil of a wakeful night she amused herself by weaving a tale, she knew nothing of it in the morning.' " Fortunate amnesia.

James Weldon Johnson and Paul Laurence Dunbar, at the end of the nineteenth century and the beginning of the twentieth, still wore the mask of gentility that Wheatley had donned in the eighteenth century, though Dunbar loosened it a bit with his dialect poems. Perhaps an agonist, a poetic theoretician, is necessary before a movement can begin, and no agonists of Soul poetry—to be distinguished from Oversoul poetry—would arrive on the scene until the 1960's with LeRoi Jones and others. Even so, the theories propounded by contemporary Black poets look much like Emerson's when they deal with abstractions, like propaganda leaflets out of Transcendentalism when they deal with social consciousness, and like the "free verse" *vs.* metered verse arguments out of Whitmania when they deal with technique.

Phillis Wheatley and Philip Freneau were contemporaries, born within a year or two of one another. In *Our Singing Strength*, Kreymborg says that Freneau "was the first American after Anne Bradstreet to follow the muse exclusively. In two centuries, two people place poetry higher than any mundane concern." Kreymborg, like everyone else, had forgotten Wheatley. Americans can boast of three considerable professional poets in two centuries.

Freneau's ambivalence was not of the classic American visionary-artistic type; he was a committed artist. Rather, his was an ambivalence of style, neo-classical versus pre-romantic. Waggoner says that Freneau "was a competent journeyman, born perhaps in the wrong time, when a style of poetry and of thinking was about to be replaced by another that would make his own seem irrelevant. Freneau had the misfortune to be a 'traditional' poet, imitative in the old mode, not yet fully aware of, or able to create, the new romantic mode." (*American Poets*, p. 30.)

There is something wrong, however, with this talk of old modes and new, transitions, and so forth. It is as though our historians are blaming an ethos, or some other abstraction, for our poets' shortcomings, rather than placing the blame where finally it must lie: our poets simply weren't very good, nor would they be until the nineteenth century. Their imaginations were limited. It wasn't the age's fault that our poets were merely journeymen, though perhaps it was the age's, or the nation's, fault that it did not encourage capable people to write poetry. It is evident there were great people in view, but they wrote in the pragmatic fields of politics or theology.

Certainly, some of our amateur poets had more imagination than did our professionals: Edward Taylor's imagination was fantastically baroque, and Manoah Bodman's simply fantastic, though it showed more in his prose work than in his poetry. To read Bodman's account of his conversations with angels and demons, in *An Oration on Death*, is to step through a mirror darkly into the world of Poe or H. P. Lovecraft, except that it comes off as real, not literary in any way; however, both Taylor and Bodman were concerned mainly with religion, which was acceptable to their society, a subject of practical concern. Neither Bradstreet nor Wheatley were particularly religious poets, except in rather conventional ways. Nor was Freneau.

Perhaps an Emersonian critic like Waggoner would say that this sectarianism was at root why our professional poets' work was of a mundane order: poetry is a religious experience, an exploration of the self and a discovery of the soul, not entertainment. What American professionals needed was an agonist to give them a sense of poetic being in a rationalist age, in a materialist nation. Given a failure of personal imagination, poets may need either a major theorist—such as Whitman found in Emerson—or at least a major exemplar who, in his or her productions, sets the standard. The amateurs found their agonist earlier than the professionals. Not until the twentieth century would the professional poets have T. S. Eliot to set over against Emerson; Eliot would, in fact, be both agonist and exemplar for the cause of poetry as artifice rather than vision.

America produced no exemplars in the seventeenth and eighteenth centuries—poets who, despite all handicaps, simply towered out of the ranks. All the exemplars were British, and our underprivileged singers could merely reflect the current poetic styles of the mother country. What poetic names can America conjure with in the nineteenth century?—Emerson, Whitman, Poe, Dickinson. These sounds have the same sort of ring as do the names Wordsworth, Coleridge, Keats, Shelley, Byron, Browning, Arnold, but what can we do with the eighteenth century? Wheatley, Freneau, Bodman, as against Dryden, Pope, Blake, Gray, Goldsmith, Johnson, Burns. If we were to try the same thing in politics or polemics it is a question whether England would so easily overshadow its colony. The American novelists of the nineteenth century fare much better than our poets. At least fiction has an obvious function: it entertains, and when America finally decided that a little entertainment was all right, Cooper read a bad English novel, decided he could do at least as well as that, and did. Washington Irving, the younger Dana, Hawthorne, Melville, and Henry James, to name a few, did likewise.

Not that nobody honored our nineteenth-century singers, merely that no one paid serious attention to them. At no time in our history were poets more honored. Bibliophiles, in their browsings through secondhand bookstores, have long been amazed to see how many editions of our nineteenth-century professional poets there are on the shelves: "Household Editions" of Bryant, Longfellow, Holmes, Whittier, even John Godfrey Saxe—the period's Ogden Nash—weight the boards. The nineteenth century cast them in amber; it institutionalized them and began to teach them in the schools, whence the term "Schoolroom Poets." Perhaps everyone in the grades still gets an annual spring-tonic dose of *Snow-Bound*—institutionalized poetic respectability. Since when has poetry been "respectable"? England didn't institutionalize its Romantics because they were respectable.

In America poetry is a matriarchal institution in every sense of the word, including the genetic: the mother of white American poetry was Anne Bradstreet; among her lineal descendants were Dana and Holmes. The mother of Black American poetry was Phillis Wheatley. Furthermore, American poetry was institutionalized by women in the schoolrooms of the nation for two centuries. These schoolmarms acted as literary censors—only that which was acceptable to "refined feminine sensibilities"—to quote from an old schoolbook—was allowed as literature. Is it any wonder that many Americans, including Whitman, grew up believing that such poetry was not "manly"?

Most important, however, is the Emersonian dogma regarding what constitutes American, as distinguished from European, poetry. Poetry "of the mind"—classical poetry—has traditionally been defined as "masculine" poetry; poetry in balance of mind and emotion—that is, formalist poetry—Emerson saw as essentially European, concerned with matters of conscious craft, artfulness. It was against this latter kind of poetry, practiced by the post-Modernists, that the Beats rebelled in the 1950's, just as it was against this kind of British poetry that Emerson inveighed. There was but one choice left for Emerson: to define American poetry as of the Soul or Oversoul—it is emotional, feeling poetry. Poesy of "the emotions" has been traditionally defined as "feminine," but even Europe has written poetry of emotion, so that would not sufficiently allow of an American poetics in and of itself. No—much Romantic poetry is artful, concerned with form and technique. What, then, is to distinguish American poetry? Intuition, of course. One need not write out the adjective almost automatically used to modify the word "intuition."

Emerson's jargon is full of words that link the writing of poetry to the processes of birth, nurture, growth. American poetry would be, then, a feminine poetry from conception to delivery. Sanford Sternlicht, a contemporary amateur poetaster, believes that, because he is not a woman and cannot bear children, he therefore "gives birth" to poems instead (*The Teaching Writer: Two Essays on Two Arts*). But one need not ransack obscurity in order to discover other examples of sexuality being equated with the creation of American poetry. In *The New Naked Poetry*, John Logan writes that "as a lover reaching out to you the audience with the long penis of my tongue of poems, showering the sperm of my syllables and breathing on you with the passion of my warm breath, I have only recently learned to look at you as you are looking at me." Fortunately, Galway Kinnell in the same volume offers an antidote to this and the various other toxins to be found between those covers. He says, with considerable insight, "There is often a deep anti-intellectualism, a lack of balance and reasonableness, even a certain stupidity in American writers."

Poetry—Emerson and his cohorts to the contrary notwithstanding—is an art, not an egg. It is the product of a human being using words in order to express his or her humanity, and the humanity of others. Words are symbolic forms, not spermatazoa. A poet is not merely "masculine"—all brain and brawn; not merely "feminine"—all heart and intuition. A poet is a whole person, whether male or female, and a poem is the artifice of the whole person. Sternlicht's theory of poetry composition is a "male chauvinist" theory: Under such circumstances, why would there be women poets at all? Women can have babies; therefore, they should have no cause to write poems. Surely, poetry is not an exclusively male product; it is an exclusively human product. No one should believe intuition is an exclusively feminine trait, nor that intelligence is masculine. The traditional definitions are arbitrary and fallacious.

Finally, the whole Emersonian argument boils down to grievances against technique. Once all the false issues of Transcendental poetic theory are laid aside, the bedrock is this: if one knows how he is writing something, he is a mechanic, but if one proceeds by intuition, he is pure of heart, a true Poet. The manner doesn't matter, only that the matter isn't mannered. Emerson, Whitman, and Waggoner are uneasy before the elements of language. When they criticize they are all right if they can theorize or generalize or abstract, but they stand amazed before the great mystery of craft, if it is successful, much as they stand in awe of Vision, if it comes off, and in disdain if it doesn't.

Writing is not birthing; composition is not foetal growth; a poem is not a babe in swaddling clothes. The analogy is a false analogy. Poetry is not feminine or masculine, black or white—it is both, and neither. American poetry is not a manifestation of mother love, it is language art written by Americans about the human experience in all its manifestations. The best poetry, regardless of where it is written or who writes it, or according to whatever theories it is composed, is words in delicate balance of expression.

This debate regarding what constitutes "American" poetry is absurd on its face. It has arisen out of jingoism and self-righteousness, out of a belief in a Manifest Destiny and out of cultural schism. What is interesting is that despite it, or perhaps because the issue was raised, the debate has given rise to agonists and exemplars on both sides, and America has in fact produced a body of poetry of impressive magnitude, primarily in the twentieth century. It is a paradox, perhaps, that much of our finest poetry is international in its significance, and that it grew out of a local squabble about poetic theory.

Our poetry seems to have taken its force, not out of a deeply rooted popular culture, but from a literary and ideological struggle among intellectuals and theologians. Even they don't particularly want to read the poems—they'd much rather argue. At the present moment in America there are dozens and scores of excellent unread poets, but for every one of them there are a hundred English teachers who do not read the poetry produced by their own generation. In the sciences, in the social sciences, in the other arts and humanities—even in theology and philosophy—teachers keep up to date, but mention Howard Nemerov, Mona Van Duyn, David Wagoner, J. V. Cunningham, to name just a few of our finest contemporary poets, and often one will draw a blank from an English teacher, even a college teacher.

Teachers are still trapped by the schoolmarm mentality and attitude toward poetry; they are still teaching the Schoolroom Poets or, at best, the Modernists of half a century ago: Eliot, Stevens, Pound, Williams, Frost. A few have worked up to Roethke, Sexton, Plath—poets of the 1950's and 1960's; one or two know a poem by Randall Jarrell or Robert Lowell or Richard Eberhart. Forget about Weldon Kees or Delmore Schwartz. Perhaps the situation is even worse than this; there was an article in *College English* in 1975 that told about a student who submitted a portion of one of the most famous contemporary poems—Roethke's "The Waking"—to an undergraduate contest, and none of the English professor-judges recognized it.

Beginning in the 1960's the hippest teachers began to bring Bob Dylan and Joni Mitchell into the classroom. Maybe, bad as it is, this new "rock culture" is the "folk" culture August Hekscher says we never had, out of which American culture might have built a deeply rooted poetic tradition. If so, it comes belatedly: a rudimentary folk art hard on the heels of a great literary art. We've always done things backward in the United States—after our Modernist Renaissance, why not slip into the New World's literary Dark Ages?

Fortunately there are too many fine young writers around; they won't forever be buried under the Emersonian caul, nor even the Beatles' larvae. Someone will read them sometime during the next century. Who knows? Perhaps someone will even begin to read and teach Bradstreet and Wheatley, if for no other reason than to prove we've had a viable professional poetry in America for a long time, and that this tradition is even older than the so-called "Emersonian mainstream" tradition that has so dominated the contemporary literary scene. That our early poetry was not very good is no dishonor—the nineteenth and twentieth centuries have made up for that. There are, however, some fine individual poems in our past, and they are being ignored because we are more interested in such things as Oversoul and theory than in art and literature. The least we owe to our foremothers is an acknowledgment of their early commitment to artistry.

American Literature as Something Else

Alfred Kreymborg titled a chapter in *Our Singing Strength* "Forefather Bryant." Though there had been other American poets before him, William Cullen Bryant is supposed to be the first true American poet because . . . he wrote about the American landscape. So did Bradstreet and Freneau. Bryant, however, wrote about it in blank verse, and nobody had done that. No, but Cowper, the Englishman, had written about the English landscape in blank verse, and Bryant as a child had read Cowper.

Bryant was concerned with Nature and Death—so was Bradstreet and the Englishman Blair, whose poem "The Grave" gave Bryant his subject for "Thanatopsis." But "Emerson and Whitman stood by him," Kreymborg says, so Bryant must have been our first truly American poet. Not only that, but Bryant "wrote a survey of American poetry of the highest significance. It was the first declaration of independence in American letters."

Emerson's address on "The American Scholar" is usually hailed as the first; but Bryant's essay appeared about eighteen years earlier. After admitting that the poetry of the past "is better than it could have been expected to be," the young author scored the prevailing slavery to English models. "This way of writing has an air of poverty and meanness . . . and it has ever been, and ever will be, the resort of those who are sensible that their works need some factitious recommendation to give them even a temporary popularity."

That proves conclusively that Bryant was American: he anticipated Emerson by flogging imitative American poets nearly two decades before "The American Scholar" was published. Never mind that Bryant's own techniques were not original, nor his subject matter, nor his treatment of his subject, nor his language, nor the ways in which he constructed his idiom—he was the first to flog decadent Europe, with its tradition of "Makers" rather than "Visionaries," so he was Forefather Bryant, the first certified American poet. Bryant wrote the Pledge of Allegiance to American Poetry, and all those who wanted to join the American Poetic Legion have had to recite the oath ever since. Tear out the pale stars of Anne Bradstreet, Edward Taylor, Phillis Wheatley, and Philip Freneau, and start clean with one true-blue poet.

One need not belabor the absurdity of this position, nor the absurdity of its continuance into the twentieth century. There's nothing wrong with scorning imitation and derivation, if the imitations don't equal or surpass their models, and if the derivations do not lead into originality. On this score Bryant comes off reasonably well; some of his poems are as good as some of the better English poems of the period—no mean feat. It can even be argued that one or two of his poems are better than almost anything written in North America up to the first part of the nineteenth century.

On these grounds, Bryant's work has true historical importance. But wouldn't it be nice if the American poetic canon consisted of first-rate poems rather than poems by historically and biographically important poets? How much more interesting, for instructor and student, if courses in American literature could be devoted to the study of the best writing produced in America.

What in the world is a teacher to tell his students about Bryant?

That he wrote "Thanatopsis"? One can spend a class period on "Thanatopsis," and one more on a few other poems, but has duty been done? No. One has not considered Bryant's historical importance—but that has nothing to do with literature, that has to do with literary history; one has not considered his life—but that has to do with biography, not poetry. Not that Bryant's life and times cannot illuminate aspects of his poetry, merely that they are, or ought to be, secondary in importance to the few good poems he produced. But in our schools biography, history, critical theory are of primary importance—they have pre-empted literature. We study the ripples rather than the stone.

One envies the scholar of medieval British poetry who is relieved of the necessity to teach the poet, for often he has no idea who wrote the poem, and even if he does know the poet's name, seldom has he much more information than that. All he has is the art object itself, and he can concentrate on it. Under these circumstances, language becomes important, as it was to the poet. The scholar must study that language to understand how the poem may have sounded, what the idioms—the very words—meant in the context of the poem. In his study he learns history—often the poem is the history—and it is manifest that the culture which produced the poem is carried *by* the poem. The poem is important; it always was, but its importance is diminished in an academic system and in a society that does not value its arts. If we have no love of or delight in our language, we turn to theoretics, history, and biography; ideas, actions, and lives. But there are already departments of philosophy, history, psychology, and sociology. Why can't departments of literature teach important literature? Even the elements of poetics? Yet we continue to teach Major Poets, not major poems.

In the teaching of poetry at all levels there is a silence regarding the most basic elements of the genre. This silence about the structure of poetry, which is the fundamental concern of the writer, proceeds from pure ignorance of the subject, an ignorance without doubt fostered by Emerson's militant anti-intellectualism where the religious subject of poetry is concerned.

In secondary school, students are confounded by teachers who have been trained to believe that there are only two ways to write poetry; namely, in accentual-syllabic, usually rhymed verse (the "British" way), or in "free verse" (the "American" way), which no one seems able to define. Although poets have been writing poems in a thousand different ways for centuries, no teacher seems capable of explaining simply what is to be seen on the page. As a result, teachers try to jam everything into traditional metrics, and when it can't be done, both teachers and students know something is wrong, but they don't know what. So the teachers pretend everything is all right and call the exceptions "free verse" or "sprung rhythm" or something equally undescriptive. At this point students turn off their minds on the subject and go to college.

In college they meet professors who also do not know the different prosodies of poetry, for no one has ever taught them, either. These instructors confuse something as basic as genre, and they cannot explain the differences among fiction, drama, nonfiction, and poetry. Poetry is the genre of language art, as distinguished from fiction, the genre of written narrative; from drama, the genre of theatrical narrative; and from essay, the genre of written argument or exposition. Thus, the poet concentrates upon language as substance, in much the same manner that ceramicists concentrate on clay as shape or dancers on the body as motion. The poet may use any and all language techniques that are available to other writers, but the purposes for which he uses these techniques is secondary to the shaping of language.

The poet may use either of two modes—prose, which is unmetered language, or verse, which is metered language. Any of the genres may be written in either of the modes; that is to say, there may be prose or verse fiction; prose or verse drama; prose or verse essay; prose or verse poetry. These distinctions between *genre* and *mode* ought to be obvious, but that people continue to confuse the two is evident in the often-asked question, "What is the difference between prose and poetry?" There is only one logical answer: "Prose is a mode, and poetry is a genre."

Item: A professor of English literature, an expert on the British poet Ralph Hodgson, knew nothing about "dipodics." He had never so much as heard the term. Dipodics is the prosody in which Hodgson wrote; it is also the prosody of nursery rhymes and folk ballads.

Item: Two other colleagues, both assistant professors, one a Shakespeare scholar and the other an African literature specialist—reluctantly admitted that neither had ever been taught to scan a poem. They could not scan even iambic pentameter blank verse, the primary metric of Shakespeare.

Item: Hyatt Waggoner himself, when challenged in a letter to come up with a definition of "free verse," replied that he could not do so given the definitions of prose as unmetered language and verse as metered language. He said he would much rather "talk about *cadenced* language." He was sent the *O.E.D.*'s definition of *Cadence*: "I. in verse and music; 1. The flow of verses or periods: rhythm, rhythmical construction, *measure* [my emphasis]." What Waggoner was talking about is the repeated stress patterns in recurring model sentence structures. For instance, in a prose sequence, the following model sentence will provide a *sense* of verse if it is repeated, because the stresses will always fall in nearly the same places:

> Cárpenters wíeld hámmers;
> Másons úse trówels;
> Ládies plý neédles;
> Bábies ríde trícycles;

and so forth. This is what Whitman does. It remains prose, however, and teachers ought to understand that it is and explain to their students that there is nothing wrong with prose poems.

Such cautionary tales might be extended indefinitely. The great

English prosodist T. S. Omond, in his book *English Metrists*, shows in considerable detail that what scholars have for centuries been saying English language poets do bears little or no relation to what the poets have actually been doing. In college, students meet professors such as these, professors who are scholars or critics for the most part, rather than writers themselves. For them *how* the poem was built is of little value—they are interested in more esoteric things.

It's as though a group of freshman were taken out into the desert on a guided tour. They come to a beautiful palace called "Poetry," which is built in the air on four marble pillars. When they arrive, the guide calls out, and someone lets down a golden ladder. The students climb up to the palace and are met by a professor who immediately ushers them into a vast baroque hall called "The New Criticism Throneroom." When they have finished there, the students visit the Freudian Wing for a time, with its loveseats and ornate couches. Then they cross a stagnant moat surrounding the Tower of Structuralist and Post-Structuralist Criticism, which has nothing whatsoever to do with structure, and nothing much to do with literature either, except with criticism for its own sake— criticism as literature divorced from literature! Perhaps they recuperate in the Transcendental Suite, full of starlight and Cosmik Muzak played through loudspeakers.

When they leave, it is night. The students climb down the golden ladder and are led blindly away—no one has shone a torch upon the marble pillars that support this marvel in the air. If someone had struck a light at the right time, the pupils would have seen plaques on the four pillars: "The Typographical Pilaster," "The Sonic Pilaster," "The Sensory Pilaster," "The Ideational Pilaster." If one had examined these pillars closely, he would have discovered how the magnificent Palace of Poetry was supported in the firmament by simple stone, the work of the craftsman and the architect.

Instead, the students clamber back into the bus, traverse the desert and, when they reach the first oasis, they are given transfer tickets in the form of diplomas. They scatter on various conveyances to the four corners of the world. Some of them become teachers themselves, and they teach what they have been taught to others who may eventually make the same journey.

The journey is a hermetic circle academically; the cycle of ignorance is self-perpetuating. In this case, however, ignorance is not bliss; it is very uneasy, and this is the reason for the silence tacitly produced in our English departments on the subject of prosody and poetics. If no one admits he is confused, no one will be found, like the king in the fable, to be standing before his class and his profession, stark naked.

On occasion students ask their professors to define the term "Great Poet," but such a phrase is useful only in the context of a class in literary history. Why not talk about great poems instead? Even minor poets have produced great poems—"Thanatopsis" may be a case in point. But if one is pressed one might reply that a great poet is one who, in a lifetime, has produced two or three or more great poems and generally maintained a high order of competence in the rest of his or her work. A minor poet is one who merely maintains a high order of competence or somehow manages to write one or two great poems although his or her level of general competence is not particularly impressive. Literature is full of one-shot poets, or poets who never quite made it to the upper slopes of Parnassus. Nevertheless, many of our finest poems have been written by minor poets, and one might better teach and study these poems than the merely competent—and sometimes incompetent—work of a putative major figure. Given a choice between Longfellow's "The Ropewalk" and Whitman's "Scented Herbage of My Breast," it is Longfellow any day, but this is not the sort of choice we get in the American classroom. Even if we do study Longfellow, we study him for the wrong reasons, and we study the wrong poems as often as not.

Bryant wrote two or three wonderful poems, and his level of competence was steady if it wasn't particularly arresting. What great poem did Longfellow write aside from "The Ropewalk" and perhaps his Civil War carol "Christmas Bells"— *The Song of Hiawatha*? No, Henry Wadsworth Longfellow was minor and derivative in every way throughout his career, and one wouldn't blink if Allen Ginsberg or some other neo-Transcendentalist wanted to rap him a few times for being nothing more than a hack imitator of the English Romantics.

Perhaps one might be a bit kinder to John Greenleaf Whittier. *Snow-Bound* is one of the few choices of the schoolmarms that can be justified as literature: it gives pleasure still. A great poem is one that does not destroy itself under close scrutiny and that continues to move us reading after reading. A great poem may have flaws, but it transcends them. *Snow-Bound* is such a poem for many people. Whittier wrote too much too sloppily to be considered a major figure, but he had his moments. "Skipper Ireson's Ride" is one of the few American dialect pieces that work as poetry, and it is a joy to read aloud.

Poe is counted by many as a major poet, and it would have to be admitted that a good many of his pieces aren't easily forgotten, though one might wish to do so. He is a peculiar figure, and his poems are even more peculiar. Given his strange and hypnotic music—so easily imitated, but never successfully assimilated and built upon by anyone else—Poe's work can probably never be dismissed, though many have tried. One can find any number of flaws in Poe's verse, but long after one has tired of ticking them off the strange rhythms and echoics of "The Raven," "The Bells," "Israfel," "Ulalume," "The City in the Sea," "Eldorado," "Annabel Lee" and many others go on kicking around in the blood. The poet-critic Daniel Hoffman almost did not have to write his book on the subject, for its title just about says it all— *Poe Poe Poe Poe Poe Poe Poe*.

Grinding our teeth, we may have to admit Poe's greatness, though he doesn't look very American to us—but what was he? He wasn't French—it was he who influenced the Symbolists, not the other way around. He certainly wasn't English, which must irritate the Emersonians no end, especially when some scholar makes the claim that Poe himself was a Transcendentalist of sorts. What we may have to say at last is that Poe was our first Flower Child in deadly nightshades.

Who else in the American nineteenth century might be considered to be "great"—Jones Very? James Russell Lowell? Frederick Goddard Tuckerman? Sidney Lanier? Herman Melville? Melville's reputation as a novelist should fool no one into believing that he was a poet as well. His fiction was his poetry; his "poetry" was something else. The same is true of Henry David Thoreau with regard to his nonfiction. Emily Dickinson is indisputably a great poet.

What about Emerson—was he a great poet? If we remember that the Emersonian dogma requires that technique is to be considered, if not totally irrelevant to poetry, at least of only secondary importance to the poem's "Vision," we may wonder why he spent so much effort in his poems experimenting with prosodies and meters, as in "Hametreya" which is partly monologue and partly soliloquy; it is a celebration of nature and a rumination on death— ode and elegy. If its setting is America, there is very little in the poem or in its style to show that this is New England, not Old. About the only thing that differentiates it from other Romantic poetry is its mixture of prosodies. If there is Vision here, it is well-hidden. There is more Vision in Wordsworth's "Ode on the Intimations of Immortality"—in fact, more Transcendental philosophy.

Emerson as an experimentalist pointed backward more than forward—backward toward the English Renaissance when everyone, seemingly, was investigating the various possibilities of the incalculably rich English language. The progression of prosodic lock-step after the Renaissance, especially during the eighteenth century, was socially inhibiting, but it wasn't only nineteenth-century American Transcendentalists who were crying out for more poetic freedom; what we need to recall is that that is what the Romantic revolution was all about. Far from severing our literary ties with England, we had merely become partners rather than apprentices, perhaps nearly equal partners, in that revolution, for our poets were getting better, though not particularly different. Even in England there were eighteenth- and nineteenth-century people who were trying "odd" things: Christopher Smart in the eighteenth century was writing poems in grammatic prosodies a hundred years before Walt Whitman stumbled upon them; Gerard Manley Hopkins in the nineteenth century was rediscovering accentual prosodies that would eventually influence twentieth-century American poets.

England made a good whipping boy, but the whipping boy was, and continues to be, largely a literary straw man. Notwithstanding our denials of the fact, our two literatures are bound together inseparably if by nothing other than a common tongue. As long as that is a truism, comparisons, influences, and derivations are inevitable, at least until communication across the Atlantic is totally severed. Even at that, it would take ages before our languages diverged sufficiently to become capable of individual literatures. Meanwhile, all we have is our nationalism and our competition.

If Emerson isn't a great poet, why do we study his work in our poetry classes? The question by this time ought to be rhetorical. Emerson was an agonist, a theoretician of, among other things, poetry. He was responsible for Whitman.

The Good Gray Poet

It was Whitman who put Emerson's theories into practice, and that is why he is considered to be a Great Poet, not because he wrote great poems and maintained a high level of competence in the body of his work. It will be objected that Whitman can be considered great on other grounds: he broke with tradition and wrote in a whole new mode which freed American poetry from the constraints of English prosody. Even if this were true, which it is not, such a defense is historical and not literary. It is a scholar's defense, not that of a writer or a reader.

That Whitman was thoroughly familiar with Emerson's work is well documented, but he need not have been. As Waggoner points out in *American Poets*, everything he required was contained in the essay "The Poet." "This is true not simply because the essay states nearly all the ideas Whitman was later to express in his poetry, or even because the essay recommends that the ideal poet should write in the *manner* of the author of *Leaves of Grass*. It is true because Emerson's idea of what a poet is and does was precisely the idea Whitman needed if he was to move beyond journalism and mediocre versifying." (P. 154.)

Waggoner is being kind. Whitman was not, in his earlier pieces, a mediocre versifier—he was simply execrable. There was no way in the world he was ever going to be able to handle the language metrically—he had a tin ear and a ham hand. Here is an entirely typical product of Whitman's early pen—not juvenilia, but an adult piece from his days as a journalist:

> Old Grimes
>
> He lived at peace with all mankind,
>   In friendship he was true;
> His coat had pocket-holes behind,
>   His pantaloons were blue.
>
> Unharmed, the sin which earth pollutes
>   He passed securely o'er,—
> And never wore a pair of boots
>   For thirty years or more.

It is all but impossible to find these early verses in any popular edition of Whitman's work, even in volumes with such titles as *The Collected Poems* and *The Complete Poems*, edited by such people as Malcolm Cowley. One must go to one of the rare multivolume scholarly editions if one wants to read Whitman as a benighted non-American, in those days when he went to social events in a top hat and cape, carrying a nob-head cane, in order to write a story for a newspaper. Later, realizing that he was a poor traditional craftsman, Whitman became the first American to discover what many others, including Emerson, were struggling to discover—namely, that poetry may be written in prose. Everyone else thought it had to be written in verse, which explains why a person such as Melville, who was also a failed versifier, was much more the successful poet in his later novels, for a succinct definition of *poem* might be this—that something said well is something well said, but something said superbly is a poem.

American and British poets were so locked into the *verse* = *poetry, prose* = *something else* syndrome that it would cause a huge ruckus in the early twentieth century, and people would go around calling prose *vers libre* or "free verse" till minds were so confused it would take half a century even to begin to sort things out. Only Amy Lowell would have sense enough in those early days to introduce the term "polyphonic prose." Meanwhile, the scholars and teachers went around trying to justify Whitman's lines as some kind of hybrid metric and, of course, it couldn't be done.

If Whitman was the first American to write straightforward prose poetry, he was hardly inventing something new. Grammatic parallelism is in all likelihood the oldest prosody in the world— the Chaldeans were using it in the *Gilgamesh* epic at the beginning of history. For that matter, the Bible—even the King James version—is written in the grammatic prose parallel systems of Hebrew prosody. As we have seen, grammatically parallel structures tend to exhibit parallel rhythms; they thus give a sense of verse, but they are much easier to write.

The fact is that Whitman was no less derivative, in his own way, than his un-American Anglophile compatriot poets. Though he could not have been aware of Christopher Smart's experiments with prose poetry because they were not published until the twentieth century, Whitman could hardly have missed the work of another Englishman, Martin Farquhar Tupper, whose *Proverbial Philosophy* appeared when Whitman was nineteen. One can still, if one digs a little, find a reference here and there to Whitman's connection with Tupper. The following passage is from *Everyman's Dictionary of Literary Biography*, edited by D. C. Browning and published in 1962:

[Tupper] wrote many works in prose and verse, only one of which, *Proverbial Philosophy* (1838), had much success. But the vogue which it had was enormous especially in America, where a million copies were sold. It is a singular collection of commonplace observations set forth in a form which bears the appearance of verse, but has neither rhyme nor metre, though its rhythms, inspired by biblical passages, are said to have influenced Walt Whitman. Tupper's name has become a byword for the trite and platitudinous.

Meanwhile, Whitman's name—because Whitman was an American—has become a byword for the innovative and oracular, not for the derivative and banal.

A million-copy best-seller in the fledgling United States! Whitman would have had to be deaf and blind to miss Tupper. It is a pity that our own great American bard of the people was comparatively ignored, according to Kreymborg, who says that *Leaves of Grass* "was intended for the divine average and the average ignored it, as to this day they ignore it. In the literature of the world, there is no greater irony, no greater tragedy, than the neglect paid by the people to a man of genius embracing the gamut of the Common American man and lifting it to a continuous chant resounding round the earth." (*Our Singing Strength*, p. 207.)

If it is true that the man in the street ignored Whitman, it needs to be pointed out that the man in the street, particularly in America, ignores all poetry, all poets. It is a segment of the educated middle class that sometimes patronizes American poetry, even if its members do not read it—teachers, students, other writers, for the most part. When it comes to this element of society, Whitman did as well in his own time as anyone else, including the Schoolroom Poets. *Leaves of Grass* went through twelve editions between 1855 and 1892, and it is still going through edition after edition. Furthermore, even Whitman's early verses had wide circulation in the pages of some of the newspapers of the day, and a *Selected Poems*, edited by Arthur Stedman, was published in 1892, the year of the poet's death.

In many anthologies of poetry published in the nineteenth century, even obscure ones with titles like *The Royal Gallery of Poetry* (1888), *Cyclopedia of British and American Poetry* (1881), and *Representative Poems of Living Poets* (1886), Whitman is well represented. He is included in nearly all the standard anthologies of the period, and he has been represented in anthologies and textbooks ever since. *Leaves of Grass* was reviewed in the leading periodicals and journals of the day, and to cap everything Emerson, the foremost critic of the period, praised his work fulsomely. What does this prove? That although Whitman was unable to persuade the common laborer to read poetry, the Good Gray Poet was, almost from the start, a member in good standing of the American literary establishment. That he was controversial merely emphasizes the point.

If Whitman was no technical innovator, and if he was no literary pariah, he was perhaps the first American poet who recognized the value of public relations as a means of building a reputation. No doubt his years as a journalist provided him with the training he needed in order to harness the medium (no one could yet use the plural *media*) and make it pull the Whitman bandwagon. In the same edition of *Everyman's Dictionary of Literary Biography* that makes the connection between Tupper and Whitman, the article on the latter says that "Whitman is the most unconventional of writers. Revolt against all convention was in fact his self-proclaimed mission. In his verse [*sic*] he established a new tradition of freedom of form and expression, while in his treatment of certain passions and appetites, and of unadulterated human nature, he was at war with what he considered the conventions of an effeminate society; but after all reservations, there is real poetic insight and an intense and singularly fresh sense of nature in his best writings."

We shall have more to say about that word, "effeminate," in the next chapter, but for now we need only notice that here is an example either of one editorial hand not knowing what the other is doing, or perhaps of scholarly split-mindedness; furthermore, almost none of this is true; we merely think it is because we have been so well-conditioned by the public relations juggernaut Whitman set rolling. We needn't talk about Tupper and the prose systems of the Bible again; we need to point out that Robert Burns in England more than a half-century earlier was incomparably more unconventional and scatological in *The Merry Muses of Caledonia*. Whitman had an instinct about how far he could go with his unconventionality without being dismissed out of hand as just another reprobate; he was unconventional enough to be fired from a government job for publishing "immoral" books, but not too unconventional to be granted another government position, which he held until illness forced him into retirement.

Whitman presented himself for duty in good public causes: he was a Civil War nurse, and he became associated in the public mind with decency and liberalism, which ameliorated the outrage some people felt over his writing. He appropriated to himself not only the prosody of one of the most popular books of poetry of his day, but also the tenets of the most influential critic of his day—he followed Tupper's prosodic formula and Emerson's theoretical precepts to the letter. To these elements he added two important ingredients: a populist credo, and a celebration of the ego. Neither of these was new, either. For the populism, one need look no farther than Whittier, who in 1833 published *Justice and Expediency* against the institution of slavery. His *Songs of Labor* appeared in 1850, five years before *Leaves of Grass*. Egopoetic verse and prose are as old as literature—both Anne Bradstreet and Edward Taylor wrote them, though Whitman could not have seen the latter's work. Whitman's celebrated "I" narrator had, however, been appearing for two centuries in America; among those contemporaries who used it were Bodman, Bryant, Emerson, Whittier, Very, and Thoreau.

Whitman was, however, an innovator in one important sense, and perhaps this is what makes the difference: he fused the populist credo and the egopoetic narrator so that the "I" of his poems became symbolic of America. In other words, Whitman *became* America, or so he would have his readers believe. By whatever means this brilliant—and brilliantly simple—fusion was brought into being and focused upon the American audience, it became almost impossible to talk about Whitman the poet, to criticize his work, without seeming to criticize America itself.

When his work is stripped of all extraneous considerations, perhaps his only intrinsically "great" poem is "A Noiseless, Patient Spider," as memorable a piece of writing as any in the language. It is also atypical of Whitman's work. The level of his competence was not very high—he retained his poor ear throughout his life; his poems are too long, too disorganized, too pompous, too repetitious, too boring; he is too determinedly, one-sidedly, un-relievedly optimistic—nobody can be that affirmative all the time. Whitman is not interested in humanity except possibly as an abstraction—there are no living people in his poems, though there are many lists of people; there are no characters except himself, and even his Self comes off as symbolic, not palpable, a two-dimensional persona.

If, however, we must look at Whitman as the embodiment of a Transcendentalist theory of literature, as a literary-historical watershed leading to all those democratic prose poems of the twentieth century, as an image of all those just and liberal and worthy things we would like to think we hold in our heart-of-hearts as a nation, then perhaps he was a Great Poet. That still doesn't make him worth reading as literature.

Masculine and Feminine in American Poetry

Walt Whitman "was at war with what he considered the conventions of effeminate society." In "A Backward Glance O'er Travel'd Roads" he wrote, "I say the profoundest service that poems or any other writings can do for their reader is not merely to satisfy the intellect or supply something polish'd and interesting, nor even to depict great passions or persons or events, but to fill him with vigorous and clean manliness, religiousness, and give him *good heart* as a radical possession and habit." These are his polarities—the effeminate and the manly.

Although he insisted, in his prefaces, that American poets were henceforth to speak for both men and women, nowhere does Whitman mention the possibility of a great woman poet. To the contrary, he had scorn for "civilized" American society. In the 1856 preface he wrote, "There is no great author; every one has demeaned himself to some etiquette or some impotence. There is no manhood or life-power in poems; there are shoats and geldings more like. Or, literature will be dressed up, a fine gentleman, distasteful to our instincts, foreign to our soil. Its neck bends right and left wherever it goes. Its costumes and jewelry prove how little it knows Nature. Its flesh is soft; it shows less and less of the indefinable hard something that is Nature. Where is any thing but the shaved Nature of synods and schools? Where is a savage and luxuriant man? Where is the overseer?"

There is a distinction to be made between the words "effeminate" and "feminine." Whitman did not denigrate the feminine—he luxuriated in it as much as in the masculine, though of course a man should be a man and a woman a woman—the two should revel in their kinds, not ordinarily adopt the qualities of the other except in particular literary circumstances. The *Oxford English Dictionary* says that *effeminate* means things like "Womanish, unmanly, enervated, feeble, self-indulgent, voluptuous; unbecomingly delicate or over-refined." These are the qualities Whitman deplored in his prefaces, but the reader who knows Whitman's work, in particular the "Song of Myself," may find certain questions presenting themselves for reflection at this point, as for instance, "Was Whitman not self-indulgent, even voluptuous?" For the moment we will defer such questions to consider the *O.E.D.*'s definition of *feminine*: "Characteristic of, peculiar or proper to woman; womanlike, womanly." The latter word is defined as "having the qualities (as of gentleness, devotion, fearfulness, etc.) characteristic of a woman."

Next, *masculine*: "Having the appropriate excellences of the male sex; manly, virile, vigorous, powerful." And *manly*: "Possessing the virtues proper to a man as distinguished from a woman or child; chiefly, courageous, independent in spirit, frank, upright." It is clear where Whitman thought the great American poet should stand. Any woman who stood on this masculine ground would not be true to her nature; therefore, a great American woman poet, from Whitman's viewpoint, is impossible.

There was, however, a worm in the apple of the New Eden: Whitman would be a poet of democracy, not of despotism; of the common people, not of the privileged and "effeminate" elite. A democratic society would possess the masculine virtues of vigor, power, courage, independence, frankness, uprightness; but it would also be capable of gentleness, devotion, compassion, openness, freedom. In order to be the Great American Poet, therefore, Whitman had to appropriate to himself the chief "feminine" virtues, as distinct from the "effeminate" vices. He would adopt all the strengths and none of the weaknesses of womankind, and this is how American woman would have her say: Whitman (and the other manly American bards, if any) would speak for her.

On the other hand, it would hardly be appropriate, even if possible, for the woman to attempt to adopt the manly virtues, for what would she then become? John Godfrey Saxe, Whitman's contemporary, stated the problem concisely in an epigram:

> A Dilemma
>
> "Whenever I marry," says masculine Ann,
> "I must really insist upon wedding a *man*!"
> But what if the man (for men are but human)
> Should be equally nice about wedding a *woman*?

If a woman adopted the manly virtues, she became masculine, but if Whitman adopted the womanly virtues, he became the Great American Poet, a feat not all American male poets were capable of, for it took a certain largeness of Soul, without which they became effeminate.

What, then, of the women who aspired to become poets? America has had at least one important, perhaps central, woman poet in each century of its existence as a colony and as a nation. Anne Bradstreet was America's first "professional" poet, in the seventeenth century; Phillis Wheatley was the first professional Black poet in the eighteenth century; Emily Dickinson is an undisputably great poet of our nineteenth century, and Marianne Moore is counted by many as a major twentieth-century poet.

What of democracy itself? The general drift of American society since Colonial days has been to let more and more people, includ-

ing women, into the "church," if one may be permitted the meta-
phor (though it is not wholly a metaphor). The movement of our
democracy, since its male-dominated Puritan beginnings, has been
toward greater openness and compassion for everyone. Real Cal-
vinism lasted only a short time, and early reformers included
women—Anne Hutchinson, for example. If openness and com-
passion are to be considered feminine traits by our culture, then
our educational system, long dominated by the presence of women
in the grade schools and built on the precepts of William James,
John Dewey and others, is a "feminine" system. As Whitman him-
self noted, the very concept of democracy combines elements of
both the manly and the womanly.

If authoritarianism is culturally equated with the worst aspects
of masculinity, it is patent that masculinity has all but been erased
from American society, except in the politics of the far right. And
if the concept of democracy is extended to the arts—which, in Eu-
rope, were never conceived of as serving the masses until the ad-
vent of Communism—then we are left with the paradox that Walt
Whitman was a man who wrote a feminine poetry, democratic in
its techniques, in the liberalist things it said, in the very audience
for which it was intended. Even the precepts of Whitman's mentor,
Emerson, must be considered feminine: loving, open, ecstatic.

In the four women poets mentioned, America has, contrarily,
produced what might be considered a "masculine" art. Before we
pursue this notion we need to identify, if possible, the poetic voice
in which a "masculine" or "feminine" poet speaks, and this voice
will have something to do with narrative viewpoint—with the
relative "objectivity" or "subjectivity" of the speaker.

Objectivity has for ages been defined as a masculine trait. In the
Emersonian credo, the idea of objectivity is anathema, as it has
been in American society in general since the 1960's. If poetry is
defined as anything at all today, it is "personal expression." On the
other hand, *subjectivity* has conventionally been identified as femi-
nine. Parenthetically, one might note that an interesting aspect of

conventions is that they may or may not be "true." It need hardly be said that men do not have a corner on objectivity, nor women on subjectivity; we just stereotype one another in order to make things easier for us to act on our irrational prejudices.

In poetry there are three possible narrative viewpoints. In every poem ever written someone is speaking. If the poet has been speaking from the subjective viewpoint about the self, the ego-poetic viewpoint has been used.

If the poet has been talking about someone or something else primarily; if, although the word "I" may appear, it is of something external the poet has been speaking rather than internal as in ego-poesy; if the poet has been telling a story about someone other than oneself, or perhaps one's own story, but maintaining a certain distance; if the words "he" and "she" or "you" appear in the main narrative, then the poet has been using the narrative viewpoint.

If the poet has been speaking from the viewpoint of someone entirely different from oneself, has projected the imagination into the personality of another individual, has adopted a poetic mask, a persona, then the poet has been using the dramatic viewpoint.

One might point out connections, though they are not absolute, of these three viewpoints with the three major subgenres of poetry, and with the three traditional kinds of poetic syntax that Donald Davie identified in his *Articulate Energy*. Many "lyric" poems are written in "subjective syntax" from the "egopoetic viewpoint"; "narrative" poems in "objective syntax" from the "narrative view-point"; "dramatic" poems in "dramatic syntax" from the "dramatic viewpoint." The primary difference between the major sub-genre of traditional lyric poetry and the contemporary minor subgenre of "confessional" poetry appears to be the forswearing, in much of the latter, of meters and rhymes and, as in Whitman, the substitution of prose parallel grammatic prosody. As Waggoner has pointed out in *American Poets*, the work of "Movement" poets such as Denise Levertov, and of "Feminist" poets like Adrienne Rich, is descended directly from the practice of Whitman.

Essentially, the egopoetic viewpoint is single-angled. It is the poet taking a stance in the center of the world of the self and telling it subjectively. It is specifically the viewpoint that Emerson requires of the "true poet," especially of the American poet. The egopoet's method is confessional in nature and exclusive in effect. There is but the one angle of vision, and either the reader does or does not agree with the poet's confession, his vision or revelation. Those who do not agree are excluded from participation in the subjective, ego-centered relation.

At first glance it would appear that Emily Dickinson in most of her poems uses the egopoetic "I," as in No. 465 of Thomas H. Johnson's edition of *The Complete Poems*, beginning "I heard a Fly buzz." Why do we assume this is an egopoetic narrator speaking in the poem? There are two reasons, one technical and one cultural, but both linked. First, Dickinson did not, in manuscript, title her poems—titles were added posthumously by her editors. A title is important in a poem; it gives the reader a context, and often it is a key to the subject. Without titles, we have to guess what Dickinson is writing about. Since Dickinson was a woman, we guess she was being subjective, and this is the cultural reason for our assumption that the narration is egopoetic. Dickinson's editors added titles, and arranged her poems in departments, on this assumption. Ever since, our minds have been conditioned to respond to Dickinson's poems in a personal way, even when the poems make no sense if they are seen as confessions or diary entries.

Looking at No. 465 we ought to ask a basic question: is Dickinson speaking? If so, how does she manage to speak from beyond the grave, since the speaker is dead? True, she might be imagining herself dead, but if so she is using the dramatic viewpoint, not the egopoetic, because she is placing herself objectively in a situation she has never actually experienced. She is but an actor in a drama of her mind. Even this, however, is not the case. Waggoner has identified the speaker as a character out of one of Dickinson's favorite authors, Nathaniel Hawthorne: the speaker is Judge

Pyncheon in *The House of the Seven Gables* describing the moment of his death as he sat in the window of his home.

Many of Dickinson's poems are still riddles, but enough are identifiable as narrative or dramatic to raise the suspicion that some of these riddles, at least, will eventually turn out to be similar to No. 465 with respect to viewpoint. Number 49, "I never lost as much but twice," is also a voice from the grave; No. 187, "How many times these low feet staggered," is an elegy to a dead housewife—the subject is not Dickinson herself; No. 448, "This was a Poet," is an elegy also; No. 449, "I died for Beauty," is the description of a dialogue by two dead people, from the viewpoint of one of them; No. 585, "I like to see it lap the Miles," has long been known to be about a railroad train, and No. 986, "A Narrow Fellow in the Grass," discusses a snake. Many others of her poems are written in the plural "we" rather than the singular "I," and others are in the second person "you," which is obviously narrative viewpoint.

None of this is to suggest that Dickinson's poems are not personal—all poems are personal to the author—nor to say that she never used the egopoetic "I"—nearly all poets do at times. It is, after all, a legitimate technique, and it appears in other genres as well as in poetry, but Dickinson was neither narrow nor exclusive; she was much broader than we have given her credit for, and more narratively concrete than we tend to think. Her poems are full of the specific, and her favorite method is metaphor. Whitman, except in his newspaper verse, is much more exclusive and abstract—in fact, nearly one hundred percent the egopoet.

And Whitman was the male—so much for the myth of subjectivity as a feminine trait. There are merely poets, and they choose their methods. Whitman chose to be narrow, to speak from a single angle of personal vision; Dickinson chose to write about everything, not just to catalog the crowds in the American streets and claim to be speaking for them, but to write of the All, from numberless angles.

Poetry requires no particular viewpoint and, as long as it is defined as personal expression rather than as language art, men and women may write as though it were merely an outburst of emotion rather than as a reflection of the whole personality. Indeed, this is exactly what happens repeatedly throughout literature. Because the products of such an ambience and attitude are unbalanced, however, most confessions—unless they are written in such a way as to captivate the reader with imagery or word music—do not stand the test of time. They look like gush to later generations, though at the time they were written they may have had great popularity for one extraliterary reason or another. The same is true, of course, of any poetry of imbalance, of exclusive effect.

That society which permits its members to perceive poetry as the art of a whole person is most likely to produce whole poets. Perhaps democracy is likelier than other systems to allow this, even though it is also democracy that encourages individuals, men and women both, to regard poetry as personal expression exclusively, unlike past systems which encouraged its men to express themselves in language and its women to play the clavier. But in the cases of women who aspire to be bards, even in a democracy there will be a terrific price to pay. In order to become whole poets—at least until very recent years—women have had to deny that they are women, in the sexual sense.

Of those four American women poets whom many consider to be central in America's literary history, only two were married and produced children, and these two—Anne Bradstreet and Phillis Wheatley—are important primarily in a historical, not a literary sense. Those two whom many count among the "great"—Emily Dickinson and Marianne Moore—were bachelor women. All four were "professional" poets in the sense that they deliberately chose to make poetry the most serious thing in their lives. They were not "amateurs" in the sense that poetry was for them an avocation or merely a means to another, more "important" end such as revelation, epiphany, or communion with a supreme being.

Of the four, Anne Bradstreet is the only one who had her vocation thrust upon her after she had already become a wife and mother: it was indulgent friends and relatives who published her first book as a surprise gift. As a result of the publication of *The Tenth Muse* she became serious about this business of poetry.

Phillis Wheatley was from childhood a poet, and she remained unmarried until she was cast adrift by the deaths of her white mistress and master—a slave, she was "freed" at the age of twenty-five or twenty-six, freed to starve, if she chose, for she had almost no training except as a poet. Instead, she chose marriage and a disastrous life of illness, poverty, children who died early, and an early death for herself. We have reason to believe she wrote very little after she was married.

Wheatley was even more objective in her poetry than Bradstreet, who was quite objective, for it is objectivity we demand in the poetry of a woman if she is going to be allowed lasting fame as an artist. It is possible that this objectivity was as much a protective mask hiding Wheatley's Negro blackness from public view as it was the product of a neo-classical, rationalist era.

Everyone knows the story of Emily Dickinson who lived in her Amherst hermitage all her life, hardly venturing out of the world of her imagination and her reading. If she kept a distance between herself and society, a shield to ward off the sometimes militant assaults upon her sensibilities by editors and others, we know that she felt no such gulf between herself and her poetry, for we have her poetics in her own words, although we have to dig for it. Here is a "found" poem, a poem put together from lines in various of her letters and conversations; it constitutes as much as we know about her thoughts regarding composition:

> Poetry
>
> Memory's fog is rising: I had a terror
>   I could tell to none—and so I sing,
>   as the boy does in the burying-ground,
>   because I am afraid. When a sudden light

on the orchards, or a new fashion in the wind

troubled my attention, I felt a palsy,
    here, the verses just relieve.
    '   I am
    small, like the wren, and my hair is bold,
like the chestnut burr, and my eyes like sherry
in the glass the guest leaves. There is always one

thing to be grateful for—that one is one's self
    and not somebody else. "We thank thee,
    oh loving Father," for these strange minds
that enamor us against Thee.
                        If I read
a book, and it makes my body so cold no

fire can ever warm me, I know *that* is
    poetry. If I feel physically
    as if the top of my head were
taken off, I know *that* is poetry. These are
the only ways I know it. Is there any

other way?
               How does the poet learn to grow,
    or is it unconveyed, like witchcraft
    or melody? I had no monarch
in my life and cannot rule myself. When I
try to organize, my little force explodes,

leaves me bare and charred. I marked a line in one
    verse, because I met it after I
    made it and never consciously touch
a paint mixed by another person. I do
not let go of it, because it is mine.

Two editors of journals came and asked me
    for my mind. When I asked them, "Why?" they
    said I was penurious—they'd use it
for the world. I could not weigh my self myself—
my size felt small to me. One hears of Mister

Whitman—I never read his book, but was told
    he is disgraceful. To my thought, "To
    publish" is foreign as firmament
to fin. My barefoot rank is better. If fame

> belonged to me, I could not escape her—if
> she did not, the longest day would pass me on
> 　　the chase.
> 　　　　　　There seems a spectral power
> 　　in thought that walks alone. I find
> 　　ecstasy in living—the mere sense of life
> 　　is joy enough. The chestnut hit my notice
> suddenly, and I thought the skies in blossom!

There is a great deal here to consider—the "self," the "mind," "a spectral power in thought that walks alone." The "sense of life," "joy"—here is a whole woman, a whole human being, writing about the condition of the world while holding herself aloof from that world in order to see it complete and write about it inclusively. It is interesting to compare this piece with Marianne Moore's poem of the same title.

Marianne Moore seems to have led the most active social life, but of the four poets she is the most objective, the most "masculine." She wrote out of what Wallace Stevens termed "a mind of winter." Waggoner says of Moore, "In most of her early work she seems to be determined to be the 'pure' poet, the completely anti-romantic poet, and the poet of the most rigorous determination to keep poetry free from the 'emotional slither' that Pound had condemned, to keep it free by concentrating exclusively on 'direct' treatment of the 'thing.'"

There is a wall of glass between the reader and the Moore poem. Although Moore is an important poet in the literary sense, not merely the historical or biographical senses, readers often find it impossible to get close to her poems. One tends to admire them from a distance, the distance she has deliberately interposed between the reader and the page. There is no body of work that is more completely "artifice" in the entire literature of our language. As Waggoner puts it:

The poet who wants to write "genuine" poetry should not, we are told [in Moore's poem "Poetry"], "discriminate against 'business documents and schoolbooks' as supposedly unimaginative. These are, after all, data, "facts" which, as Pound had said, it is the business of poetry to give us. The role of the imagination in the poem is limited to the shaping of "facts" into a sort of ordered structure: genuine poems "present for inspection, 'imaginary gardens with real toads in them.'" Those who do not ask *this* from poetry are not interested in poetry, we are told flatly, but in something else presumably, something not "genuine." Perhaps not even Pound has more sharply denied any cognitive function to the imagination. We may think of Williams' "No ideas but in things" as similarly positivistic and anti-idealist, but though it is also meant to aim a blow at "high-sounding interpretation" and transcendental nonsense, it at least leaves the poet free to find the "ideas" in "things," while Miss Moore's definition of genuine poetry leaves him only the craftsmanlike function of shifting the "real toads" around to make some sort of pattern. No more stringently self-denying definition of poetry has ever been made by an American poet. (*American Poets*, p. 366.)

"Self-denial"—emphasis on the *self* again, as in Dickinson above. This is the price American society has exacted of those four women poets who, in our history, have managed to become important language artists. The sad thing is that the necessity for this self-denial may not even have been a conscious thing on the part of these women, merely a requirement of the culture. In the case of Moore some evidence may be adduced to support this suggestion, for in 1968, in response to a review of her *Complete Poems* in which egopoesy had been discussed in its contra-relationship to her work, she wrote:

The Pathetic Fallacy—Ego.
Something I have not thought about in connection with myself but have we not suffered from it day by day!

In order to create their art, these women had to become more objective, more "masculine" than any man. Only men could get away with writing a "feminine" poetry and still be taken seriously—Walt Whitman is the prime example.

Now let the reader enter into an act of the imagination: imagine that Walt Whitman is a woman. If Whitman had been a woman, and if this woman had written the self-same poems we have now in *Leaves of Grass*; if the egopoetic narrator of these poems had declared, "Who touches this book touches a woman"; if she had said,

(1)
I celebrate myself,
And what I assume you shall assume,
For every atom belonging to me as good belongs to you.

I loafe and invite my soul,
I lean and loafe at my ease . . . observing a spear of summer grass.

(2)
Houses and rooms are full of perfumes . . . the shelves are crowded with perfumes,
I breathe the fragrance of myself, and know it and like it,
The distillation would intoxicate me also, but I shall not let it.
The atmosphere is not a perfume . . . it has no taste of the distillation
. . . it is odorless,
It is for my mouth forever . . . I am in love with it,
I will go to the bank by the wood and become undisguised and naked,
I am mad for it to be in contact with me.

—If a woman had written this, would we consider her to be the Great American Poet? Would we say that she put into words what America is all about? Would we celebrate ourselves in her celebration of herself? Would we say she speaks for all American men and all American women?

We would not. Only a male poet is allowed to write like this, out of a "feminine" sensibility, in a "democratic" society. If a woman had written these lines most people would call them gush, not art. We operate on an artistic double-standard in this country. Men may write either prose confession or language art and have their productions called poetry, but women may write only the latter, not the former, if they are to be taken seriously as artists.

The contemporary Feminist poets are insisting at this very moment that their artless confessions, derived ironically from a male "role-model," be granted the same consideration and status that the productions of their master and his minions—most of them male also, like Allen Ginsberg and the other Beats—have been accorded; that democracy be extended to women's egopoetic writing and that open, compassionate, tender, one-sided personal expression be counted as language art.

Those who value Whitman's work for whatever reason, who believe with Emerson and Whitman that American poetry should not be artful or "literary" in any way, may one day find it in their souls to practice what they preach and begin to value women's confessional writing, read now largely if not nearly exclusively by instructors or students in women's studies courses. But others, if they are to be consistent in a view of poetry as lyric expression as well as personal expression, may eventually come to insist that all poets, whether male or female, be artists of the whole as well as prophet and seer. Perhaps they will not want to judge poetry according to who wrote it out of what program or political theory, nor according to its "historical" importance or the sex of the author, nor out of what movement the poem is derived; they will wish to judge a poem, perhaps, by what it says about the human condition, and by how well it says what it has to say.

The American Novelist as Poet

It appears that many American and British novelists have drawers full of poems. Once they are established as writers of fiction, out come the poems for publication, or sometimes they begin as poets and eventually settle on fiction. Hemingway, Faulkner—even that arch-realist James T. Farrell—wrote poetry, but perhaps the most striking case in American letters is that of Herman Melville.

The novelist-as-poet syndrome has often been associated with psychic agony. A fair amount of this pain is unnecessary, as we have suggested earlier, for it is caused merely by a cultural-technical confusion about the nature of the genre of poetry. Ever since the Middle Ages, English literature has been captive to the belief that poetry must be written in the mode of verse. Perhaps the crucial moment in history was when scholars took medieval manuscripts of Anglo-Saxon origin and began breaking the solid blocks of script into lines of accentual verse.

Originally, there was no literary distinction made between narrative art and language art; any scholar will say that the origin of the novel is the epic, which is now considered to be a form of poetry. It is equally a form of fiction, which is only another way of saying that fiction and narrative poetry were once the same thing.

The origins of both genres are in oral tradition. In all the cultures of the world literature was composed in certain constructions according to particular conventions, no doubt at least in part because such structures were easy to memorize and to improvise. In European literatures authors composed according to verse prosodies—syllable-counting systems; in other oral literatures, however, conventions of the same sort were built on grammatic parallels rather than syllable metrics, and the mode used for both the genres of fiction and poetry was prose rather than verse—this is the burden of tradition of the oldest literatures in the Western world beginning with the Sumerian epic of *Gilgamesh* and extending through the Old Testament.

The oldest Anglo-Saxon manuscripts were transcripts of oral literature. Scribes simply wrote down, in long lines without artificial breaks, the songs, stories, homilies, or whatever else they heard and wanted to record. On paper now for the first time, what the scribes wrote out looked like prose. Later, when scholars got to analyzing these manuscripts, they detected conventions that seemed to be metrical. By the time the printing press had been invented, the accentual prosody of the Anglo-Saxons had been deciphered, even though they themselves had never seen these pieces of literature on a page, or even envisioned them in terms of discrete lines.

The scholars who edited these manuscripts for publication for the first time laid out Anglo-Saxon literature in "stichs" or lines so that the metric would be obvious to the reader who, after all, wasn't necessarily familiar with Anglo-Saxon oral traditions. Whole new conventions had been established in English literature in the intervening centuries, from the introduction of French syllabic verse in the eleventh century and the invention by Chaucer and his contemporaries of accentual-syllabic prosody in the fourteenth century. With the advent of printing, literature took on a dimension as something to be seen on the page as well as, or instead of being, heard by an audience.

At this point an ambivalence of mode took root in English literature, and the appearance of the prose novel at about the same time complicated the problem. People began to believe that fiction ought to be written in prose, and poetry in verse; soon, verse narratives came to be perceived not as fiction but as poetry, and a burden of tradition that included a genre/mode confusion was built into our literature. Furthermore, fiction was perceived as the genre of mass entertainment whereas poetry began to accumulate a reputation as the genre of serious literature and elite endeavor. It is no wonder that Whitman, whose desire was to reach the common man, returned to prose as the vehicle for his poetry.

Melville, however, wanted to write "literature" rather than entertainment, and he seemed not to be much interested in continuing to reach the mass audience that had read his early novels. Inasmuch as he was as confused as everyone else, he therefore assumed that he had to compose in verse in order to write poetry, though his talent lay elsewhere. It evidently never occurred to him that, at least in his later novels, he was writing a true poetry, and in his "poetry" he was merely versifying "deep thoughts," as in his epic-length *Clarel*.

Melville was an inward-looker, an explorer in the area of experience and belief, a man who would be true to what he had experienced, whose philosophical dilemma was that he had also to be true to what he believed. Melville was as incapable of reconciling these spiritual opposites as he was the ambivalence of mode, even though the necessity to do so threatened to sunder him. He could not understand how a logical, ordered universe could exist when experience indicated chaos was the order. Therefore, Melville got into the habit of seeing the fact, "normality," and behind it the

horror, the bone-chilling heartlessness of the "ocean"—deep, im-
ponderable, unpredictable. This was his major subject, and he
wrote about it in both prose and verse.

The merging of opposites which, in melding, would not lose
their separate identities was the central motif of his creative life.
He carried it in embryonic form through his early novels of the
sea, to full maturity at last in the amalgam and monument of all
his various literary experiments, *Moby Dick*, an epic novel. That
this was not an unconscious process, though mystical; that it did
not slip into his work in any unknowing way, may be seen if we
examine the entire body of his theory of creativity, the poem
"Art," which is an example of Melville at his versifying best. The
poem is an attempt at definition.

Written in fairly strict iambic tetrameter couplets with an
unrhymed line—line seven—inserted, this poem is as much as
Melville had to say on the subject; he preferred to create rather
than ask questions of the mysterious process of creativity:

> Art
>
> In placid hours well pleased we dream
> Of many a brave unbodied scheme.
> But form to lend, pulsed life create,
> What unlike things must meet and mate:
> A flame to melt—a wind to freeze;
> Sad patience—joyous energies;
> Humility—yet pride and scorn;
> Instinct and study; love and hate;
> Audacity—reverence. These must mate,
> And fuse with Jacob's mystic heart,
> To wrestle with the angel—Art.

Though Melville was as much a mystic as Emerson, this credo is
a far cry from the exclusive Transcendental definition of poetry as
Vision alone. Flame and ice, or passion and intellect, must "mate."
They themselves remain intact, but that to which they give birth
will be a fusion. It will be art—poetry. They will fuse in an enigma,

that "mystic heart" Melville could not name, as Poe named it, where anomaly-and-anomaly may become fact in some inexplicable way.

Melville was something more than a metaphysician, however; he was also a word-lover, as all language artists are. He would fondle individual words and strike sounds together in order to find what echoes might be set ringing. In his novels those words could gong like buoy bells in the long tides of prose, but in his verses, unfortunately, they often sounded merely odd or archaic. Note his use of "lones" and "off-hat" in "The College Colonel"; "ice-cubes," "jack-straw," "sliddery," "methought" and "lubbard" in "The Berg"; "saw-pit," "charnel" and "ravener" in "The Maldive Shark."

Sometimes, however, Melville used words in strange, imaginative, and effective ways in his verse. For instance, in "Malvern Hill" the image, "Does the elm wood / Recall the haggard beards of blood?" is striking, expressive, but in context it is more than strange, it is jarring. Though the language of this passage is what might be termed "modern," the language of the rest of the poem is archaic, typically romantic in the derogatory sense of that term— "Pinched our grimed faces to ghastly plight" stands out as typical of the total poem. It is pompous, stilted; its strict rhyme scheme, long-short line alternation, ponderous language, trite (even in Melville's day) battlefield-heroic subject matter, all militate to make the "poem" an almost total failure. Here is another example of a burden of tradition weighing down the writer; in this case, the tradition is that poetry must be composed not only in verse, but in a poetic diction, a syntax different from, more "elevated" than, ordinary language.

But the poem is not quite a failure because the last stanza is beautiful and simple. Somehow, the burden of tradition fell briefly from the novelist's shoulders, and he became for a moment a poet who respected but did not venerate the language, who managed the fusion he called for in "Art." Melville addresses the trees on

Malvern Hill, anthropomorphises and asks them romantic, bitter questions about the sights they had "seen" during the battle. Suddenly, succinctly, directly, the elms answer:

> *We elms of Malvern Hill*
> *Remembered every thing;*
> *But sap the twig will fill:*
> *Wag the world how it will,*
> *Leaves must be green in spring.*

In "The College Colonel" Melville chose as his subject a young man who has had his boyhood snatched from him and been given instead the experience of the battlefield, with its fears and responsibilities. He has been wounded, overwhelmed by reality, yet he has won through; we see him returning to the cheering throngs of home. But the cheers mean nothing. They are empty, significant of no fact that the young colonel has experienced. It is an unreal world, this world of life, for death was, is, too close under the surface. It is much closer than the blind and deaf society of peace cares or dares to admit.

In this poem Melville utilized the title itself as the first line; "He rides at their head" is the next line to follow. The Colonel, then, is at the front of those who have returned. "A crutch by his saddle just slants in view." The use of the word *slants* is interesting, well-framed. Thus, in two lines and a title we have the whole scene, most of the exposition. This is succinct language.

The meter is rough, irregular. The rhyme scheme is variable. Melville let the requirements of his meaning govern his form. He was not above using consonance in place of rhyme in order to allow the meaning its full scope rather than fetter it with the strict traditional forms he found so hard to handle. Melville was no master of accentual-syllabic verse technique, though he was better at it than his contemporary Whitman had been.

As in Whitman's prose poems, those elements of Melville's language that presaged our contemporary diction—such as the line "An Indian aloofness lones his brow"—seem out of place in con-

junction with such unnecessary (considering the freedom of met-
rics Melville left himself) antique expressions, inversions, and
stilted phraseology as, "but to *him*—there comes alloy"; "Self he
has long disclaimed"; "A still rigidity and pale." But perhaps it is
too much to ask that a poet throw over completely the burden of
tradition that weighs upon his era, although there are those who
have done it, including another novelist-poet of the period, Ste-
phen Crane.

Melville grounded "The College Colonel" solidly in the specific,
as he did in many other poems and as might be expected of a
storyteller, but the "metaphysical" conclusion to which he pro-
ceeded, the crux and climax of the poem, is nothing more than the
ambiguous romantic statement, ". . . there came— / Ah heaven!—
what *truth* to him." This is the Romantic moral tag of nineteenth-
century poetry, a device Melville did not use in most of his later
fiction. He was able to allow the ambiguities and paradoxes to
stand in his novels, stand and speak alone of the nature of man and
his circumstances, without comment. In a good many of his poems
Melville sounds more Emersonian than in his stories. An annoying
aspect of visionary "Truth" out of Emerson by Transcendentalism
is that it often turns out to be abstract and unusable, and Emer-
sonian poets tend to be unable to describe or even name the
quality or nature of their truth. It seems to be enough for them
merely to claim they have it, and surely that should be enough for
the reader. It is not, at least not in "The College Colonel."

"The Berg," subtitled *A Dream*, is one of Melville's most am-
biguous poems both thematically and structurally. It is variably-
rhymed at random; its metrics are irregular—partly loose iambic
tetrameter lines with now and then a pentameter inserted. It is
reminiscent of some of Emerson's poems, such as "Hametreya."
Portions of the language are interesting, perhaps even brilliant,
but the poem contains its fair share of anachronisms also. The
ship might be symbolic of two or three things: Man, or man's intel-
lect, or the foolish belief in an artificial reality. The berg itself

might be nature, or truth, or perhaps another manifestation of Moby Dick, for it too is huge, white, afloat in the sea, imponderable and deadly. The poem is plainly symbolic, but it is not close enough to allegory for the symbolism to be clear.

We have, then, the solidity and the fluid; the whale or berg, and the sea. The berg is immovable and shapeless, most of it is hidden under water; and we have the brave, foolish "ship of martial build" which, though steered against the berg, "Directed as by madness mere," could not ". . . budge it, though the infatuate ship went down."

> Hard Berg (methought), so cold, so vast,
> With mortal damps self-overcast;
> Exhaling still thy dankish breath—
> Adrift dissolving, bound for death;
>
> .   .   .   .
>
> Impingers rue thee and go down,
> Sounding thy precipice below—
> Nor stir the slimy slug that sprawls
> Along thy dead indifference of walls.

Man, or some aspect of man, brings up against the hard, impenetrable, dream-destroying fact the universe has put in the way. Life is one thing, death is another, yet they are the same, parts of a whole.

"The Berg" is ambiguous but not obscure. It has a strangely undreamlike quality about it: the scene is minutely described; all action is related. In other words, the language and structure do not support the dreamlike impression Melville seems to be after. The overall sense of the poem is merely one of equivocality, an effect that is further heightened by Melville's infatuation with sonority and alliteration, especially too near the end of this poem, in lines thirty-two and thirty-three:

> Though lumpish thou, a lumbering one—
> A lumbering lubbard loitering slow,

which serves to introduce a ludicrous note just before the otherwise strong last couplet.

> Nor stir the slimy slug that sprawls
> Along thy dead indifference of walls.

In some lines Melville had the language delicacy, judgment, and balance a poet must have, but in far too many lines, and in whole poems, he had a tin ear and a tendency to overdo the sonic level.

It is another enigma how "The Maldive Shark"—stupid, horrible, instinctual, deathbearing—depends upon the lively, "sleek little pilot-fish, azure and slim" to guide it to its prey. Yet the smaller fish, safe and secure among the shark's very teeth, "never partake of the treat" of the "Pale ravener of horrible meat." Here again opposites converge yet are not changed one by the other. The result is terrifying, yet factual; orderly, and illogical.

"The Maldive Shark" is as close to perfection as Melville ever came in his verse poetry. Even the superfluity of adjectives in this poem, though certainly no indication of an economy of language, is not particularly obtrusive, for Melville is otherwise direct. His subject is a shark and its guides, which he described in sixteen lines. There is only one syntactic inversion, in line four: "How alert in attendance be." He works directly from the concrete description to the anomaly of horror guided by grace.

Reality and dream must mate if one is to produce art, Melville said, and in "The Maldive Shark" he finally managed to produce in verse a work of art. Neither reality nor dream eclipses the other, and balance is maintained in the language of the poem. If there is a flaw here, it is in metrics: the rhythms tend to be sing-song, and the penultimate line breaks the meter awkwardly.

Melville attempted in his verse poetry, as in his prose fiction, to depict the solid setting for the couchant dreamworld which reality must reveal to the eyes and mind of the inward observer, but at least in his verse Melville's attention to detail, jagged meters, and overblown poetic diction tended to overbalance his observation in favor of the concrete image and at the expense of symbol. Together with his juxtaposition on the one hand of an archaic and, on the other, of a curiously twentieth-century vocabulary and syntax, these faults confuse the reader and divert attention from the ambiguities Melville tried to illuminate.

Why was Melville a successful illuminator of ambiguities in his novels and an unsuccessful wrestler with technique in his poems? Why are so many novelists unable to write poetry; conversely, why do so few poets make decent novelists? Howard Nemerov gave the answer once at a writers' conference: to write a novel, one needs a novel idea. (Some writers, of course, are successful both as poets and as novelists. Among contemporaries, one might mention Nemerov, Joyce Carol Oates, and David Wagoner.)

In other words, the writer of any genre needs to identify what he or she must concentrate upon; the novel is generally a form of narration, and its language, therefore, is primarily a vehicle for that narration. The novelist's concentration must be upon the story, and the story will illustrate the idea behind the plot—the theme.

Poetry, however, is language art, not narrative art. The intensity of the poet's focus must be on the language itself, as we have argued earlier. If the poet is successful, the elements of language itself—the rhythms, the images, the wordplays and sounds—will illustrate the theme of the poem. Melville tried to pummel the language of his poems to serve as a vehicle for his ideas, as he used language to serve as a vehicle for his stories. In his prose he gave himself up to story, but in his verse he never learned to give himself up to the language.

The Eve of Modernism

Until 1912, when Harriet Monroe was about to found *Poetry* in Chicago, thereby giving Ezra Pound and Modernism their first major forum in the United States, American poetry had been "imitative and derivative," a sub-branch of British poetry for two and a half centuries. Only one or two poets had been exceptions to this rule. Ever since Bryant, though some American literati had been kicking against the traces, most had been unable to break away from traditional accentual-syllabic metrics in practice, including Emerson, the agonist for a new poetics. Most of the trouble seemed to be technical—American poets had difficulty in getting personal voices out of the old forms. Emerson prescribed a remedy: invent new forms; cast off the burden of tradition and allow American poems to grow naturally, like plants; operate through intuition in order to attain Vision, which is poetry's core, and the form will follow "organically."

If Whitman took the medicine, no one else did in Victorian America—but suddenly, at the turn of the twentieth century, there didn't seem to be a problem for three American poets who continued to write in the old forms. Edwin Arlington Robinson began to emerge from the shadows; Robert Frost published a few poems in periodicals; and Ezra Pound himself issued *A Lume Spento* in Venice in 1908—"A collection of stale creampuffs," he was to call it in 1964, "at a time when Bill W[illiams] was perceiving the 'Coroner's Children.'"

Perhaps so, but Pound was gamboling about in medieval Provençal forms like a dolphin in its native element. Not many years later e. e. cummings could be so confident of sonnets that he would disguise them by means of grammatic dispersion, and he would be considered an extreme Modernist by baffled traditionalists, rather than the sentimental romantic he was. At the Library of Congress' National Poetry Festival in 1962 Langston Hughes, talking about his early years as a professional poet, could even assign pecuniary motives to this kind of confident, cavalier treatment of verse: "Well, I learned long ago—and I tell you young people this, many of you are going to be poets and hope to sell your poetry—I learned long ago to take a four-line poem and cut each line in half and make it eight. You get a little more." It was Langston Hughes who codified and established as a literary form the native American blues poem.

How did it suddenly happen that, after such long agony, Americans could become master technicians who were also fine poets? It wasn't because form itself was so difficult to master, though it is difficult enough, of course—many American poets from Anne Bradstreet on had been adequate technicians; it was because Robinson, Frost, Pound, and others had been able to relieve themselves of the burden of tradition associated with formal poetry, but without discarding the forms themselves.

The Emersonian phobia about "form" is reborn with every American poetic generation. Kenneth Rexroth wrote in the anthology *The New Naked Poetry*, "Socially viable patterns, like conventional verse, are a sort of underwriting or amortization of the weaknesses of the individual. There is the kernel of sense in the hollow snobbery of Valéry. The sonnet and quatrain are like the national debt, devices for postponing the day of reckoning indefinitely. All artistic conventions are a method of spiritual deficit-financing."

If this means anything at all, it means Rexroth had no notion of the meaning of "artistic conventions." All elements of language, including the sounds of the syllables, the letters of the alphabet, the words and their arrangement in sequences, are both forms and conventions. No communication is possible without conventions—people must agree on the meanings of sounds and on how those sounds are arranged, in forms. A sonnet is no more or less formal than a sentence; though it is more elaborate, perhaps. Still, the word "form" raises the hackles of poets like Karl Shapiro who, in the 1960's, was writing prose poems and resurrecting the perverse claims of the British Romantic novelist Thomas Love Peacock to the effect that, not only was formal poetry dead, but *all* poetry was dead inasmuch as it was nothing more than the infantile nursery songs of the race, and mankind had outgrown its cradle and nursery rhymes. Once again the British had anticipated the American revolutionary, and all Shapiro could do was repeat, and quote, ideas a hundred years old. He did not mention that Peacock sometimes sneaked poems into his novels. Later on Shapiro himself went back to writing sonnets.

American poets are forever announcing that "the sonnet is dead," but the sonnet cannot die, for it was never alive. It is nothing more than an abstract pattern. If one can disencumber himself of the associations he has attached to the sonnet, the form remains waiting to be used in a new way. It is neutral, as every "system" is neutral until it is applied. Every little old lady in tennis shoes, of either sex, from Truro to Hilo, has written a sonnet—people like Louis Ginsberg, Allen Ginsberg's father, and perhaps Allen himself who, astonishingly, in 1979 published in *The American Poetry Review* rhymed and metered poems that were every bit as bad as his father's.

Every garden club poet has written a triolet, one of those Provençal forms Pound was juggling nonchalantly in the first decade of this century. It is the form which Edgar Lee Masters derogated in his poem "Petit the Poet." The burden of its tradition is that it is a pretty little thing, fit only as a vehicle for writing about fluffy cloudlets on a spring day and daffodils in a meadow. Even Dylan Thomas, when he was a child, wrote a "Triolet" and fell under the weight of the burden of tradition. It isn't a poem at all, and it might be assumed that it was such youthful failures as this that turned Thomas in his maturity away from English metrics toward his native, more ancient, Welsh syllabic prosody.

Even so, it is a strange fact that, at a particularly poignant moment in his life—when his father was dying—Thomas again turned to a closed Provençal form to write one of the most famous villanelles in modern poetry, "Do Not Go Gentle into That Good Night." Assumedly, when he wrote this poem Thomas wasn't thinking of anything but his father and the poem being composed, and the burden of tradition simply didn't exist at the moment. Even Theodore Roethke, paradoxically, would use the villanelle form in "The Waking" to enunciate Emerson's central thesis about "organic" poetry: "I learn by going where I have to go."

Long before Thomas wrote his elegy and Roethke stated Emerson's credo in a traditional form, Edwin Arlington Robinson had written another famous villanelle, "The House on the Hill," not to mention any number of sonnets and other poems in strict forms— poems that could have been written by no one else. They were original and true works of art. Not that Robinson didn't borrow elements from other writers—Robert Browning, for instance, in his psychological portraits of people, and Hawthorne in his balance of light and dark. In fact, it would seem that Robinson's way was to be so conscious of craft and tradition, know them with his mind so well, that he became their master, not they his, a lesson Melville, for one, never learned.

Perhaps both ways work sometimes: If one is unaware of any

tradition, how can it weigh one down? The trouble is, how does one remain ignorant if he wants to become a poet? Perhaps one can reachieve ignorance, as Frank O'Hara seems to suggest in *The New Naked Poetry*: "I don't believe in god, so I don't have to make elaborately sounded structures. I hate Vachel Lindsay, always have; I don't even like rhythm, assonance, all that stuff. You just go on your nerve."

There were only two notable American poets before the twentieth century for whom the burden of tradition seemed to be no problem: Manoah Bodman at the turn, and Emily Dickinson at the end, of the nineteenth century. It may be possible to explain the former along the lines of Julian Jaynes in his 1977 book *The Origin of Consciousness in the Breakdown of the Bicameral Mind*. Bodman was so busy talking with devils and angels in his hallucinations or bicameral visions, and so worried about the state of his soul, that he could very well have been oblivious to tradition. As a result, he was writing an individual poetry, full of colloquialism and consonance, long before anyone else in America:

> Enoch and Elijah
>
> Enoch and Elijah both went up to heaven,
>   Their journey so swift, their chariot so strong;
> And with the Apostles perhaps they are even,
>   Their wonders were great, their triumphs are long.
>
> On fiery wheels of shining bliss,
>   They rode aloft beyond the skies;
> For they have gone where Jesus is,
>   Where the bright cherub swiftly flies.
>
> Translated mortals soar above,
>   And speak Christ's name in endless praise;
> Immanuel is endless love,
>   Then shout it everlasting days.
>
> The wonders of the cloud,
>   And wonders of the rainbow;
> The wonders of the flood,
>   And wonders of the rain too,

Shall fill our souls with sweet amaze,
While we on heavenly riches gaze;
And with seraphic ardor blaze,
And from our minds all fears erase,
    Of our eternal woe.

Abram the wise, the holy and prayerful,
    And the great friend of God;
The great the father of the faithful,
    Is washed in Christ's blood.

He too, shall tell us of his holy apparitions,
His wonderful doubts and wonderful decisions;
Bright angels the instruments to tell him the same,
And all of it back'd with the Eternal I AM.

Paul and Moses both shall join,
And each their sacred souls combine,
    To read the Jewish law;
Such wond'rous lectures bright and clear,
From darkness, doubt, and sin and fear,
    On earth we never saw.

Emily Dickinson certainly wasn't unaware of literary tradition, though. Evidently it didn't matter to her what anyone else was doing. She simply reached out for forms to one of the books handiest to her in her Amherst home (as evidently Bodman did also), an Isaac Watts hymnal, and wrote most of her poems in common measure or short couplet. So much for a burden she didn't need. It was her cavalier model as much as anyone's that enabled Pound's and Amy Lowell's "Imagistes" to maintain that the sensory was the most important level in poetry.

For one brief moment, before the impending Modernist movement eclipsed nearly everything else, something existed in America that had never existed before: there were true Makers in the New World, craftsmen who knew how to build a poetry of balances in traditional European forms, yet a poetry that no one could mistake as anything but native. It wasn't American with a red-white-and-blue capital *A*, as Emerson asked for and Whitman delivered, it was simply excellent American poetry in the bardic tradition.

Professional poetry is the longest tradition in the history of American art, dating from Bradstreet. Waggoner and others date the amateur tradition from Edward Taylor, though he was unknown as a poet until the twentieth century. Although the professional—or, to use the British term, "bardic"—line antedates America's amateur tradition, we have seen that the latter was the first to produce both an agonist—Emerson—and an exemplar—Whitman. Emerson gave the movement its philosophy and critical "system" (which we will look at in a later chapter), and Whitman gave it a major voice while the American bards were still struggling to adapt traditional European methods to the New World's situation, experience, and voice. Those few bards who were technically proficient seldom managed to write an "American" poem, while those who were metrically inept were struggling unsuccessfully with the New World view in verse, but managing to get it quite often in their prose.

The bardic system was easily outshone by the Emersonians—if their accomplishments for the most part were not greater than the best professional poetry, they nevertheless got most of the headlines, and their legend in retrospect looms larger than life. The amateurs got most of this publicity because they declared for a "democratic" poetry. The bardic tradition has always been "elitist." Responding to arguments that traditional poetry is dead in America, Howard Nemerov, in his essay "The Difficulty of Modern Poetry," has remarked that poetry, like chess, is most alive when it is in the hands of masters, not "when [it] becomes altogether too easy, too accessible, runs down to a few derivative formulae and caters to low tastes and lazy minds."

That may seem un-American, but, as Kreymborg said, the masses do not read poetry, not even the poetry of Whitman, bard of the common man. Simply by writing in the genre of poetry Whitman himself became an elitist—the love of language is not a common trait, no more than the love of chess or opera.

Quietly, without exemplar or agonist, the American bards had been perfecting their craftsmanship, their visions of reality, their personal voices, and there they were in the pre-World War I years, writing beautifully and easily. Kreymborg said, "The Robinsonian ear is faultless. . . . Rarely, if ever, does he break the rules, the so-called laws of versification. He accepts the white or black pieces like a chess-expert, and having concluded one game, takes the opposite side of the board and starts another. There is no element of luck in chess, no such element in the poet."

Kreymborg was a very perceptive early critic; Robinson's work, he continued,

is compact neither of light nor of darkness, but of light and darkness, and of other supposed antitheses of the human mind: faith and skepticism, tragedy and comedy. He sees each part in relation to the whole, and is therefore the first of American tragi-comedians. A tragi-comedian is the subtlest and most difficult of men to comprehend, and the haze which greeted Robinson was due to the continued immaturity of the American mind. (*Our Singing Strength*, pp. 297ff.)

If the American reading public had difficulty in understanding the moves over the black and white squares of the psychic chess-board, it is nevertheless especially in this balance that the bards and novelists of America found what they conceived of as the heart of America. Robert Frost said in a letter to Lawrance Thompson, "Emerson's defect was that he was born of the great tradition of monists. He could see the 'good of evil born,' but he couldn't bring himself to say the evil of good born." Nor could his followers.

There is precisely the difference between the bards and the visionaries. America's professional writers had for two centuries been trying to enunciate the dance of death and darkness in the midst of blazing light. The first great professional poem in American letters, Bryant's "Thanatopsis," turned to nature and saw there the ambiguity and the tensions between opposites in the paradox of being human. But it was not yet time for the bards to make this existential dichotomy conscious—Bryant spliced an uplift tail onto his vision, as the age demanded, and even though it dangled there awkwardly, his readers could not see because America was, and is still, psychically at war with itself; in the nineteenth century the nature of the battle was not even vaguely clear. America wanted to believe it was the last best hope of the world; it wanted, and still wants, to believe that the People are righteous and uncorrupt—the opposite of the stereotypical Europe that Puritan and later immigrants had escaped. America was hope, promise, and a new slate upon which the human spirit would at last be writ in great script. Few could bring themselves to admit that being Americans was not better than being mere human beings, like Europeans and Africans and Asians.

Thus Bryant could look at the fields and woods of New England and say, after a brave start, that one would have much company in death, for earth is "one mighty sepulchre."

> The golden sun,
> The planets, all the infinite host of heaven,
> Are shining on the sad abodes of death,
> Through the still lapse of ages.

In no sense are these heavenly hosts the choirs of the righteous the Calvinists looked forward to with "a sure and certain hope"; they are the cold, flaming stars lost in dwindling space.

> All that tread
> The globe are but a handful to the tribes
> That slumber in its bosom.

Mother Nature seems distinctly unmatronly among such lines: ". . . the dead are there: / And millions in those solitudes, since first / The flight of years began, have laid them down / In their last sleep—the dead reign there alone, / So shalt thou rest, and what if thou withdraw / In silence from the living, and no friend / Take note of thy departure? All that breathe / Will share thy destiny."

The dead are alone, but not lonely; if there is loneliness in being alive, and in dying alone, take comfort in the knowledge that everyone is in the same boat. "Plod on, and each one as before will chase / His favorite phantom." His favorite phantom—we live alone with our illusions, with our romantic solace which, finally, does not cover the bleaching bone.

Though each of us is "a brother to the insensible rock," Bryant could say in the same poem—say with a straight face and not be thought a fool by his contemporaries—"sustained and soothed / By an unfaltering trust, approach thy grave, / Like one who wraps the drapery of his couch / About him, and lies down to pleasant dreams." Be Sybarites of darkness. Walk on your lonely grave by day, and by night pull your Turkish winding sheet about you. Lie down, dust, with your brother stone, beneath the stars like sand in the glass of ages.

Thoroughly un-American, if you *think* about it. If you don't, if your conscious mind hears only the uplift while your unconscious mind goes its own irrational way, how thoroughly American. If Bryant had lived in the twentieth century, his name would have been Wallace Stevens.

One can pull example after example of this kind of split-minded composition out of nineteenth-century American poetry—poems that unwittingly say one thing and prove the opposite. Some of these poems are among the greatest the age produced; often such a poem is the *only* great poem a poet produced. There is Longfellow's "The Ropewalk," for instance, and even Whitman stopped shouting his upbeat Transcendentalist propaganda long enough to write "A Noiseless Patient Spider."

In the early years of the century America was not yet far enough away from its Victorian furniture to be able to hear clearly, but Robinson and Frost had separated themselves from the century in which they had been born and were doing consciously what

American bards had been doing unconsciously since the beginning—they were taking into consideration man as a creature of darkness as well as a spirit of light. This wasn't a new thing in literature—it had been done the last time in the English Renaissance; it was being done again on the eve of the Modernist renaissance, and America for a little while was to have a poetry of conscious balance.

The American reader, however, would go on for a long time believing that Frost and Robinson were new versions of Whittier and Longfellow, nice New England country gentlemen with good thoughts and an eye for the landscape, though it *was* a little hard to stay deaf to Robinson's song of failure. It was only an aberrant type who, in the midst of Horatio Algerian success, "Went home and put a bullet through his head" like "Richard Cory"; or who took the less drastic route into alcoholism like Eben Flood (and *there* is a pun of light and dark) in "Mr. Flood's Party"; or who simply escaped into the past like "Miniver Cheevy." Much less likely was the rationalist method "Cliff Klingenhagen" worked out to cope with a reality that was at least half bitter: take bitter medicine to find joy in life.

If this was not a Whitmaniacally superhuman poetry, it was at least a less one-sided, more likely, less hysterical, more human and humane poetry. If this poetry stood in direct opposition to the Emersonian doctrine that Thou shalt hear no Evil, see no Evil, speak no Evil, it addressed the actual human condition.

If these humanist poets used traditional metrics rather than the grammatic prosody of Whitman; if they saw more than one side of the human condition, they also used poetic voices specifically denounced by Emerson in his essay "The Poet"—denounced by omission. Robinson and Frost went into the Other rather than into the Self; they understood that one can come to know oneself by seeing in other people those human qualities that lie dormant in one's own personality. The voice of the Visionary poet is the ego-poetic "I." Robinson and Frost used the narrative and dramatic viewpoints—they projected themselves into the personalities of others and spoke, like Dickinson, from the multiple angles of the race. The bards' definition of *vision* would include "world view," which would never do for Emerson—"cosmic view" was the least possible definition.

Unfortunately for Robinson and Frost, neither was an agonist; each was merely a superb artificer, but a bard was on the scene who would shortly co-opt humanist art and transform it into modernist art. Paradoxically, Ezra Pound—as great a master of craft as any poet ever born on these western shores—would live all his creative life abroad, but he would have so much energy that he would practically single-handedly transform America into a garden of Parnassian blossoms and weeds. A still greater paradox: this revolution would come to pass not because Pound was a poet, but because he was a dilettante; not because he possessed insight into humanity, but because he was a mover and a shaker among the lettered. The revolution would be set in motion by the type of poet Emerson most despised—a man "of poetical talents" but no soul. Fortunately, the forces Pound unleashed led now and then to the development of true bards. If this hadn't happened, if we had merely Poundians rather than humanists, we might all be living in cabins at Brook Farm.

The Age of Pound

The day will come, if it hasn't already dawned, when we will call the Modernist period "The Age of Eliot," but it should be called "The Age of Pound," if we must call it an "age." Because literary "ages" are given their names by scholars, and because most academics are interested less in literature itself than in such things as sources, schools, movements, biography, influences and so forth, we generally have each literary "age" named after a "major figure" rather than the best writer of a period. The last age named after its best writer was "The Age of Shakespeare." The succeeding period was filled with minor writers. Some of them are "minor" only by comparison with the Bard of Avon; still no one dominated the era with his talent, and no one has since.

What began to happen at the end of the seventeenth century in "The Age of Dryden" was that incipient Prussianism set into the universities, and the study of literature became the study of something else: literary history, great ideas, the rebirth of humanism. This trend was institutionalized in the nineteenth-century United States when Germanic scholarship hypnotized American scholars;

it has held them entranced ever since. "The Age of Dryden" was followed by "The Age of Pope," "The Age of Johnson," and then "The Age of Wordsworth." At this point, evidently, great literature ceased being produced in the United Kingdom, and "The Age of Whitman" ensued.

The poetry of these writers in no way eclipsed the poetry of their contemporaries in the same way that Shakespeare's or Chaucer's had done. Dryden was a rather uniformly bad writer. He is the father of an Age because his classical ideas won out in the eighteenth century. Pope took up these precepts and became a literary dictator—historically significant, without a doubt, but fortunately his hegemony did not prevent others, including Blake, from writing many better poems than even Pope's best. No doubt for this reason academics tend to abstract Blake from the eighteenth century and place him, uncomfortably, somewhere in limbo between The Age of Johnson and The Age of Wordsworth as a so-called "pre-Romantic." Both Blake and Burns (also typed as a pre-Romantic) were products of the eighteenth century, and it seems willfully obtuse to ignore two of the greatest writers of the period when that period is given a name.

It is patent that Samuel Johnson was not a great writer; his most famous work is a dictionary, and his second most prestigious production is *The Lives of the Most Eminent English Poets: With Critical Observations on Their Works*. The single most famous book of literature of that period was written by James Boswell: *The Life of Samuel Johnson*. Why isn't the period called "The Age of Boswell"?

Boswell and Johnson were an excellent team, and with them began "The Tandem Ages"—those succeeding periods which required two writers to fill the shoes of one. This system was brought to perfection by Coleridge and Wordsworth, kept at its peak by Emerson and Whitman, and allowed to begin a swift decay with Pound and Eliot. The system was comprised of an agonist, who was primarily the theoretician of the team, the other half of which was the exemplar, the person who wrote most of the actual poems. Though the exemplar's best poems were not necessarily better than the best of his partner, he took most of the credit and had the age named after him exclusively. The best poems of Coleridge the agonist are better than those of Wordsworth the exemplar of the Romantic era. Many of the most awful poems in the anthology *The Stuffed Owl* (a true monument of twentieth-century scholarship which is completely ignored except by nonacademic readers) belong to Wordsworth.

The system of The Tandem Ages began to crumble with Pound and Eliot because Pound was a frenetic agonist. Essentially a dilettante, though he could be both a master poet and a superb craftsman, Pound never stayed intellectually in one spot long enough to develop a coherent and comprehensive literary theory. He had more energy than anyone since Shakespeare, who was playwright, actor, director, manager, and—for all we know—ticket taker of The Globe.

Pound took all the world as his stage, and he became so busy discovering the new poets of Modernism, beginning such movements as "Imagisme" and "Vorticism" in Europe and exporting them to America, helping to transform poets of the Celtic Twilight into Great Modernists, editing magazines and other people's manuscripts, delivering himself of broadsides in various causes, and dipping into other ages and cultures, that perhaps it is a wonder he had time to write any poems at all, let alone become a philosopher of poetics. As a result, nevertheless—and it was a result—we had our American poetic "renaissance."

Looking back on the period just before and after World War I, one sees Pound everywhere, doing what seems to be everything. The times may have been ripe for the Modernist explosion, but Pound was its fuse and detonator. If history and biography are more important than literature, then Pound's age should be called by his name. Perhaps it would be, if he hadn't become a Fascist propagandist during World War II. Expatriatism has never been held against any American writer—indeed, it was a Modernist lodge requirement—but America does not forgive ex-patriotism.

Even at that, though Pound wouldn't have his age, he did have his privileged dispensation: in the history of the nation he is the only native writer to have been officially banished. The mechanism by which this act was accomplished is an interesting one, and its precedent is ominous, but it *was* a special arrangement for Pound who would otherwise have had to be tried as a war criminal. Accomplishment now and then has its rewards.

Perhaps because Pound was so busy with other things Eliot had to become his own agonist. He thus destroyed the delicate balance of the Tandem Age system by reverting in part to the ancient Major Figure system—"in part" because, though T. S. Eliot is the putative author of the great poem of the Modernist period, *The Waste Land*, those early dark rumors of Pound's heavy editing of the original manuscript have proven to be incredibly true.

One could argue that a single instance doesn't prove a point, but Pound was more than one poet's teacher. Would there have been the Yeats we know and love without Pound? Would there have been an Amy Lowell, or a William Carlos Williams, or even a Marianne Moore, of whom Waggoner wrote, "Though H[ilda] D[oolittle] is usually singled out as 'the' Imagist, that distinction, such as it is, ought rather to go to Marianne Moore" (*American Poets*, p. 364).

Kreymborg—poet, editor, mover and shaker like, and contemporary with, Pound—wrote that "Pound had fled his native land as early as 1908. . . . He was soon followed [in more than one sense of the term] by other 'expatriates'—H.D. [the initial-pen-name was Pound's invention], John Gould Fletcher, T. S. Eliot. Amy Lowell also appeared on the scene and ultimately took over the reins of Imagism [which Pound thereafter called "Amygism"]. Imagism, born in the capital of the British Empire, was destined to open the civil war in American poetry." (*Our Singing Strength*, pp. 33ff.) Kreymborg discusses the birth of Imagism at some length.

He talks about Pound's connections with T. E. Hulme, Remy de Gourmont, "the supreme critic of estheticism"; his friendship with Yeats, "another who drank at the moonlight springs of Symbolism" along with Eliot; and his associations with Ford Madox Ford, Richard Aldington and others, all of which "radically changed the course of American poetry." Kreymborg speaks of Pound's roles as literary propagandist, discoverer and champion of "unknown originals," his connection with many periodicals in the U.S. and abroad.

Kreymborg reported that the Eliot association was early and organic, but despite Pound's activity Eliot soon became the guidon-bearer of Modernism for the "Lost Generation," at least partly because he seemed "more mysterious" and owned an "excathedraic tone"; further, "After the romantic outburst of the free verse movement, poetry needed a severe synthetic critic. Next to Eliot's classical prose, Pound's read like jargon." Eliot became "the high priest of letters."

Kreymborg saw early and clearly what others have seen late, if at all. Many of these observations, even when they were seen and known, were for years suppressed or ignored throughout the "Age of Criticism," so-called by the New Critics and their academic minions while they were making a case for the proposition that literature had to move over and make room for criticism itself, now at last an equal partner with imaginative writing. We had been building to this situation ever since Johnson, who, because he was a scholar and lexicographer primarily, and a wit to boot, had become the honorific "Dr." Johnson. An autodidact, Johnson nevertheless exemplified all those things academics hold to be true and beautiful; namely, theoretics, attention to supportive (if selective) detail, research, and didactics.

It was not Pound's criticism that influenced his generation of writers nor, finally, was it Eliot's, even if Eliot's theoretics deeply affected criticism and literary study. It was Pound's explosion of scattershot from the blunderbuss of his practice that influenced, and continues to influence, poets of the twentieth century. Pound never asked anyone to do what he wouldn't do himself, and it appeared that there was nothing he could not do. Although the publication of *The Waste Land* created a gigantic stir, no school of Eliotic poetry was founded thereby.

No more need be said here about the Modernist poets on whom the mark of Pound has been set; nor, perhaps, of the influence he had on such diverse schools of poetry as the "Academic" poets of the 1950s, who followed his early formalist practice; the "Beats," who repeated Pound's cry to "Make it new!" and the Black Mountain School whose leader, Charles Olson, was called "the poor man's Pound." Pound, Eliot's *"il miglior fabbro"*—the better maker—is still a well as deep as the world, and poets continue to bring up out of his crafty depths the clear waters of inspiration. This is no exaggeration. Pound is not through influencing us. American poets today and in the future will plumb his depths to find freshets that will continue to define and redefine American poetry both experimentally and traditionally. No matter which path or paths we take, we are likely to see a shadowy figure up ahead beckoning us on.

The Waste Land *Revisited*

Anyone coming to literary consciousness after 1923 must at least confront, if not come to terms with, the problem of *The Waste Land.* It is not enough, however, merely to address the poem; one must also consider its context: the manner of its writing; the scholarship and speculation that is a direct outgrowth of the poem and of the critical writing of the poem's "author"; the time in and out of which it was written; and, finally, the lives and ambitions of Pound and Eliot.

There will be immediate objection to the listing of this last concern, for the "New Criticism" tells us that the life of an author ought to be irrelevant to an evaluation of the intrinsic worth of an artifact. Perhaps so, and it is also likely that the criticism written by a poet—in this case Eliot—will be self-serving. It would be ideal if every poem could be judged objectively, but pragmatism must win over literary idealism, and it is clear that certain works of literature are so tangled in biography and history that it is impossible for anyone to separate the artifact from the artificer and his or her times. *The Waste Land* is such a poem.

One can remember when one first began to doubt Eliot's serious devotion to poetry as a profession and to suspect him of incipient scholasticism; it is also possible to recall when he redeemed himself to a degree. If one had been born as late as the mid-1930's, perhaps one read "The Love Song of J. Alfred Prufrock" and "The Hollow Men" in the early 1950's and was as enchanted as Eliot's contemporaries must have been. Then one read *The Waste Land*—and Eliot's own notes on the poem. The Notes seemed enigmatic, the poem itself scarcely less so. It was obscure, confusing, pretentious, pompous, artsy-craftsy (Pound had left his mark, though one was still innocent of such carnal knowledge). Both, however, had their effect, but the Notes in particular, the effect of outrage. What kind of poem needed all these Notes to explain it, particularly Notes by the author? If he were a poet, not a scholar, wouldn't he have put the information of the Notes into the poem?

Even at that, the Notes helped not at all in one's understanding of the poem. It was a big puzzle, and if one felt that poetry is humanity's finest communication, *The Waste Land* seemed a waste of amorphous proportions. One did not know how to respond to it; it was unlike anything one had encountered to that date, except possibly the poems of Wallace Stevens.

Eliot redeemed himself somewhat when eventually he repudiated the Notes. By that time, however, one was beginning to lose one's innocence, and the rumors that he had included them as printer's fillers seemed credible, but what kind of serious poet would play games with what was purported to be a serious poem? There were evidently only two alternatives to consider: either the poem was a joke, or it had been written by a madman. As it turned out, neither was correct, though the second possibility came close—*The Waste Land* had originally been a sequence of short poems, old and new, made up of heroic couplets and neo-Symbolist fragments pasted together by a man in the midst of a nervous breakdown and then edited to half its length by modern letters' foremost "man of poetical talents." No wonder W. C. Williams described *The Waste Land* as a literary atomic bomb.

That Eliot is truly a great poet has always been open to dispute; that he was a great scholar-critic perhaps is not, but that may have more to do with mere reputation than anything else, as Kreymborg was quick to note. Perhaps Eliot sensed such an argument might be raised against him, for though he came within an ace of taking his Harvard doctorate in philosophy, he backed off at the last moment. One wonders whether Eliot, unlike Johnson, might have felt that to be called "Dr. Eliot" would tend to obscure his true vocation. Degree or not, he helped to usher in "The Age of Criticism."

All these suspicions and awarenesses did not spring to bloom suddenly in one's adolescence; they glimmered and flared, perhaps, during the college years and after until Valerie Eliot's edition of *The Waste Land: A Facsimile and Transcript of the Original Drafts Including the Annotations of Ezra Pound* was published in 1971. Everything was exacerbated thereby; it was the final imbalancing stone fitted into a teetering inverse pyramid.

How was one to cope, not only with suspicions confirmed, but with Valerie Eliot's introduction quoting letters in a chronology that showed the sheer manipulation that went into establishing *The Waste Land* as the central document in the canon of Modernist poetry? The deal that Pound, Eliot, and Quinn worked out with the editors of *The Dial* so as to garner *The Dial* prize for Eliot? The commissioned review written by Edmund Wilson? The self-publication of his poem by Eliot in his British magazine, *The Criterion*? Sheer public relations work, all of it.

It was not, however, enough simply to condemn the poem along with literary politics. One was no longer only a disillusioned adolescent, after all. Is there some intrinsic value in *The Waste Land*? It was necessary to find out, either to bury the poem as a creation of publicity, or resurrect it and live with it. How to go about this reappraisal was the problem. F. R. Leavis pointed a direction.

In his 1932 essay titled "T. S. Eliot," republished in 1950 and 1960 in his book *New Bearings in English Poetry*, Leavis made an analogy in several places between the process of *The Waste Land* and music:

A poem that is to contain all myths cannot construct itself upon one. It is here that *From Ritual to Romance* [by Jesse Weston] comes in. It provides a background of reference that makes possible something in the nature of a musical organization. [Mr. I. A. Richards used the analogy from music in some valuable notes on Mr. Eliot that are printed in an appendix to the later editions of *The Principles of Literary Criticism*. (Leavis's note)].

*   *   *

All this illustrates the method of the poem, and the concentration, the depth of orchestration that Mr. Eliot achieves; the way in which the themes move in and out of one another and the predominance shifts from level to level.

*   *   *

The unity the poem aims at is that of an inclusive consciousness: the organization it achieves as a work of art is of the kind that has been illustrated, an organization that may, by analogy, be called musical.

Leavis talks about musical "method," "organization," and "orchestration," all valuable terms; but in an essay titled, peculiarly enough, "Imagism and Its Consequences," from his book *Reflections on a Literary Revolution* (1960), Graham Hough extends the analogy:

The poem that abandons the syntax of narrative or argument and relies on the interplay of "themes" or the juxtaposition of images according to the mysterious laws of poetic logic is not, so far as it is doing anything positive at all, doing anything that poetry has not done before. Clustered and repeated images, contrasts or echoes among them, a half-heard music of this kind has always been part of poetic effect. We have always partly known it, and modern criticism has done much to make it explicit. But in all poetry before our time this music has been background music. What we have heard with the alert and directed attention has been something different. It has been a story, or an argument, or a meditation, or the direct expression of feeling.

If Leavis is talking about the "musical" or perhaps in this case the *symphonic* structure of *The Waste Land*, Hough means something else when he uses the term "syntax," and mentions "narrative," "argument," "meditation," and "direct expression of feeling." Furthermore, we must be clear that when he speaks of music, neither critic is talking about sonics or "language music" effects such as rhyme, meter, consonance, alliteration, and so forth. Rather, Leavis may be harking back to and expanding upon theories of the symphonic structure of poetry, such as those propounded by, among others, the nineteenth-century American poet Sidney Lanier.

On the other hand, in the paragraph quoted above Hough means what Donald Davie discussed in his book *Articulate Energy* (1958) where five kinds of poetic syntax were isolated. The first three kinds are, and have always been, standard in English language poetry; what is more, they are closely related to the sorts of narrative viewpoint that Eliot described (rather poorly) in *The Three Voices of Poetry* and that were earlier called in these pages "egopoetic," "narrative," and "dramatic."

When Hough mentions the syntax of "an argument, or a meditation, or the direct expression of feeling," he is talking about the syntax Davie calls *subjective syntax*: "Poetic syntax is *subjective* when its function is to please us by the fidelity with which it follows the 'form of thought' in the poet's mind."

Hough does not distinguish, as Davie does, between narrative and dramatic syntax: "Poetic syntax is *dramatic* when its function is to please us by the fidelity with which it follows the 'form of thought' in some mind other than the poet's, which the poet imagines." We have seen, in our discussion of Dickinson's use of viewpoint, that dramatic syntax can also be confused with subjective syntax if we do not know whether the author is using a persona when speaking in the first person singular.

Hough's "syntax of narrative" is called *objective syntax* by Davie: "Poetic syntax is *objective* when its function is to please us by the fidelity with which it follows a 'form of action,' a movement not through any mind, but in the world at large."

The main thrust of the Hough paragraph is to describe the

fourth kind of syntax, identified by Davie as *musical*: "Poetic syntax is *like music* when its function is to please us by the fidelity with which it follows 'a form of thought' through the poet's mind *but without defining that thought*." It is the contention of Davie and Hough that musical syntax has been used in twentieth century poems primarily. The argument Davie uses to defend the analogy with musical composition is basically this:

When a composer invents a piece of music, he has an "idea" that he wishes to express, but that expression must be delivered in an abstract mode: notes, tones, timbres, and so forth do not have "meanings" attached to them in the same way that words do. Thus, the elements of the composition, the notes, follow "a 'form of thought' through the [composer's] mind . . . without defining that thought." If a poet uses words in the same way that a composer uses notes, then he is writing in musical syntax.

Several American poets who have used musical syntax in the twentieth century come readily to mind. Perhaps the clearest example, apart from Eliot (with Pound) in *The Waste Land*, is Wallace Stevens. One poem in which Stevens explicitly used not only musical syntax, but expanded upon the analogy with music, is "The Idea of Order at Key West." Two later poets also come to mind—Frank O'Hara and John Ashbery. In his introduction to O'Hara's *Collected Poems* (1971), Ashbery makes much of the fact that O'Hara was influenced more by contemporary music and art than by poetry. The theory behind abstract art has more in common with the theories of music composition (O'Hara was educated at Harvard as a musician and composer) and musical syntax (at Harvard O'Hara also began to write poems) than with traditional artistic and poetic theories—to avoid confusion with language-music techniques, perhaps Davie's "musical syntax" ought to be replaced with the term *abstract syntax* by analogy with abstract art.

Ashbery himself has often been attacked on the ground that

people find it difficult to "understand" what it is he is getting at in his poetry. Eliot and Stevens were similarly attacked, not to mention Pound, but if one understands that these poets often wrote in musical syntax, not in the three standard types traditionally found in English-language poetry, then we must see that our frustrations arise, at least in part, from our unfamiliarity with abstract syntax and our consequent disorientation.

But did Eliot in fact write his poem in abstract syntax? Perhaps partly, but not entirely, and he was evidently not conscious at first that he'd done so. Pound, however, saw what Eliot had nearly wrought. As Leavis pointed out, the analogy with music goes beyond syntax into structure. *The Waste Land* is constructed like a symphony—it has "movements" or strophes. In these movements themes and motifs occurring in earlier segments are picked up, transformed, muted, dissolved, and the poem "exhibits no progression . . . [it] ends where it began."

To examine the *Facsimile and Transcript* is to be rendered incredulous. Never before in the history of literature—in English, at least—has one important poet submitted to this kind of wholesale editing by another poet. Even more astonishing is that Pound was in nearly every instance correct in his judgment. The original poem could in no way have been considered "symphonic." It was more often a music hall performance. It had transitions and introductions, often in poor neo-classical heroic couplets—these Pound excised utterly. If anything at all is clear about *The Waste Land* it is that the poem had two authors, not one. Pound had as much to do with its making as Eliot, who was being only just when he called Pound, in his dedication, the better maker.

What, however, is one to do with this information? How do we come to terms with such a precedent-shattering situation? For one thing, we ought at least to insist that all future editions of the work bear the names of both authors. For another, we ought to look for precedents, not where there are none, in literature, but where there are, in music. It is not at all unusual in music for a composition to be written by one composer and orchestrated by another. The great example of this sort of cooperation is "Pictures at an Exhibition." Record jacket notes written by Irving Kolodin for the album *Moussorgsky-Ravel: Pictures at an Exhibition* (1954) read,

It is conventional to speak of a musical experience as the outcome of an interaction between artists of two kinds: a creator and a recreator. Modeste Moussorgsky's *Pictures at an Exhibition* is unique, perhaps, in being the end product of a chain reaction involving no less than four individuals of exceptional gifts: Victor Hartmann, the artist, and Moussorgsky, who was inspired to interpret Hartmann's pictures in a series of piano pieces, were the generative two; Maurice Ravel, who gave them new life in the orchestra, is the third, and the director of the current recording, Arturo Toscanini, is the fourth.

It was Pound who recognized the indwelling musical syntax and structure of Eliot's composition; it was he who cleared away the detritus of subjective and objective syntax that obscured the basic word order and the symphonic form; it was he who junked the transitions and brought to light the emerging and receding motifs and themes. Pound's editing was a singular act of genius. Eliot's second act of composition was equally compelling: he had the in-wit to sense that Pound had transformed what came close to being doggerel, in the uncut version, into something of value. It seems unlikely that two personalities such as these will ever again come together to produce such a work of poetic composition and "orchestration," to use Leavis' term. For one thing, it is difficult to imagine another poet being as generous as Pound, or as ego-suppressing as Eliot.

Only the Notes remain to rankle, and even here one might advance a theory, though it can probably never be proved. Although the Notes should never have been written, and one could believe Hugh Kenner when he said, in *The Invisible Poet: T. S. Eliot* (1959), "The notes got added to 'The Waste Land' as a consequence of the technological fact that books are printed in multiples of thirty-two pages.

"The poem, which had appeared without any annotation whatsoever in *The Criterion* and *The Dial* (October and November, 1922, respectively), was in book form too long for thirty-two pages of decent-sized print and a good deal too short for sixty-four. So Eliot . . . set to work to extend a few notes in which he had identified the quotations."

However, when one thinks it over, it is difficult to believe that a printer's problem was sufficient motivation for Eliot to expand his Notes. Not only does one doubt it was simple expediency, but one further disbelieves that it was a cynical literary joke—that wasn't Eliot's style, nor his sort of humor. Why, then, would Eliot submit so willingly to this sort of self-serving pseudo-scholarship, which might (and nearly did) reobscure the value of the poem Pound had taken such pains to salvage and clarify? And why did Eliot eventually repudiate the Notes that had, for so long, been associated with the poem?

Perhaps the matter can be explained this way: though Eliot had the wit to understand that Pound had done him a great service through his orchestration of *The Waste Land*, it may be that he was troubled by all that cutting, unable to grasp completely, at the time, the principles of abstract syntax and structure. It was Pound, after all, who had been trained to a degree as a musician (he even wrote an opera, *Le Testament*), not Eliot, whose set of mind was philosophical, therefore predominately rational rather than associative. If much of the literary establishment was baffled by *The Waste Land* in its published form, why should not Eliot have had reservations?

If he did; if he missed the transitions and explanatory, narrative passages of the original version at the same time that he recognized how inferior they were to the portions Pound had left intact, might Eliot not have been easily tempted to restore some of these things in scholarly Notes? Perhaps Eliot was not entirely at ease with Pound's version of his poem, at least at first.

It may very well be that it took Eliot as long a time to get used to his *Waste Land* as it took some of his readers. When at last he had tuned his ear to the arrangement Pound had imposed upon his score, Eliot dropped the trappings of rationalism and let the orchestra sing unencumbered by Notes.

A Modernist Coin

Wallace Stevens and Conrad Aiken exhibit the two faces of a Modernist coin, the existentialist and the humanist respectively. Waggoner made the comparison: "Aiken never *sounds* like Stevens," he wrote, "early or late. The similarity of the two exists only on the thematic level or—what amounts to the same thing in the end—shared symbolic images" (*American Poets*, p. 477). What the two poets shared, however, was not so much a symbolism or an imagery, but the objectivity of the professional poet. Neither was interested particularly in the use of poetry as a genre for "vision" in the Transcendental sense, or for vatic experience. Such poets tend to use the egopoetic voice in their poems.

Aiken and Stevens used narrative and dramatic voices; each invented personas, donned masks in order to say what they had to say, but Aiken never forgot that he was an artist of the human, not an architect of abstractions like Stevens, especially in his late poems. Aiken was essentially a romantic; Stevens, though he looked like a romantic in his early poems, was in fact more an Aristotelian, more a poet of the mind, even than Pope.

In a certain way Stevens appeared to be an Emersonian, but he was at the opposite pole from Emerson. Earlier in these pages three kinds of poets were discussed, professionals, amateurs, and agonists. To recapitulate, professionals are those poets who have dedicated their lives to the writing of poetry; amateurs use poetry as a vehicle or a means to a larger end, such as the achievement of a religious experience. Agonists are poets who spend much of their time constructing and embellishing a particular theory of poetry. Often an agonist will write a few poems but many essays— Coleridge and John Crowe Ransom come to mind.

On occasion, however, an agonist will work his theoretics out in poetry rather than essay. Wallace Stevens is the most obvious example of this kind of agonist in the twentieth century. He spent his entire creative life writing poems about poetry, and he looked like an Emersonian because, though he was unable to believe in God and religion, he would substitute for them a system of aesthetics.

In his earliest poems Stevens appeared to be one of the fallen angels because, rather than propound his system logically, he "argued" by example, and the syntax he chose as his vehicle was abstract syntax. One had to develop "a mind of winter," or of objectivity, so that one could enjoy whatever there was in life to enjoy—primarily the life of the mind itself—without falling victim to wish or romantic despair.

The life of the mind is indeed an abstract life. In order to write about these abstractions, Stevens had to invent a set of "objective correlatives," to use Eliot's term. More simply put, each abstraction must be made concrete by means of a metaphor; the subject or "tenor" of the metaphor would be an abstraction that equalled an object in the physical world, and this object would become the "vehicle" that carried the burden of the metaphoric equation. Meaning would rise out of an understanding of this symbology, out of an understanding of what each object stood for, and how it operated in the context of its environment of other objective correlatives. By these means Stevens could build what seemed to be a solid world, but behind this world would stand, not the "ideal" world of Platonic and Transcendentalist doctrine, but the "real" world of the mind which the poet inhabited existentially.

In the early poems the objects Stevens chose to represent his ideas were often tropical or subtropical. As a result, Stevens appeared to be some sort of Polynesian Prince of Delights, and Kreymborg could write in his defense:

Stevens is more than a dandy, a designer, an esthete. Each of these persons is a phase of a central person, each a mask in a masquerade at the heart of which philosophy and tragi-comedy view the world with serenity. If the earth is a tawdry sphere, America a tawdry land, the relation of human to human the most tawdry of all, Stevens refuses to despair. Nor does he satirize the situation. He may seem superior to his surroundings; one may suspect him even of snobbery. But he is neither a misanthrope nor a snob, but one of the wisest and subtlest of natives: an American reared on French Symbolism, on the philosophic poetry of the artistocratic Jules Laforgue. Not to mention an older race: the aristocratic Elizabethans. Again we are in the presence of an enigma.

Stevens' poems are "notes,"

but what notes these are. They are among the perfect things in any literature: perfect in sensation, color and sound, versification, whether in old or new forms; perfect in language, the relation of phrase to phrase, vowel to vowel, consonant to consonant. Emotion has achieved its thought, thought its system, system its poetry: a poetry now clear, now vague, as clear and vague as life. Behind the veils, there is always a meaning, though the poet employs super-subtlety for veiling the meaning as well. No one knows better than he that all these things have been felt and thought and known before. One can only improvise on materials used over and over again, and improvise for oneself alone. Here is no question of pleasing anybody. Here is no question of pleasing even the ego. (*Our Singing Strength*, pp. 500ff.)

This passage is full of insights into Stevens and his poetry, and Kreymborg saw early what others have seen late. It was Stevens' contention that there is no meaning in existence beyond whatever meaning the artificer—the "creator" with a small *c*—imposed upon the chaos of the physical universe. In the beginning was The

Word, but The Word was not with God, whom Man had created, it was with man (with a small *m*) who is the creator of all words, including the name of God. The order of reality is the order of syntax as arranged by the mind of the artificer. Stevens' "system" posited art as the substitute for religion which had been discredited as a plausible alternative in the objective, scientific twentieth century. The name of God had lost its meaning; therefore, God no longer existed. Other names must be invented if one were going to survive chaos. In effect, then, Stevens was an evangelist for a new kind of salvation—salvation through poetry. Only imagination and the creations of imagination had meaning and reality, whereas physical "reality" was without order; hence it was ephemeral.

As Stevens grew older he traveled farther north in his poems, both geographically and metaphorically, till at last the landscapes of his poetry are austere. He was simplifying his objective correlatives, reducing to essentials the dogmas of his substitute for religion. Inasmuch as he was an agonist-evangelist, he wanted to build "a larger poem for a larger audience." If this were to occur, his ideas would have to be accessible to more people; therefore, simpler. Perhaps this would explain his later bareness, but it might better be explained in another way.

Stevens was a strange evangelist caught in a stranger situation. If reality existed only in a particular mind, then all other minds did not exist. One wrote poetry—as Kreymborg noted—for oneself, but not even for one's ego; one wrote for one's own mind. The system could be worked out only in terms of the Self; there was no use in writing for others. Stevens realized this, and in fact he did write largely for himself. It was often difficult for editors, such as Kreymborg for one, to get Stevens to send them poems. Stevens' first book, *Harmonium*, practically had to be dragged out of him. Once the system had been worked out, though, why keep on writing? Because Stevens was a professional poet, dedicated to writing, so he wrote the same poem over and over again.

If Stevens were ever to admit that other people had a valid exis-
tence in terms of the poet, then the system would be destroyed; it
would prove to be invalid. Yet repeating oneself to oneself forever
was useless, and evidently the self-evangelist felt an impulse as he
grew older to reach out and give his system to others. As soon as
they touched it, as soon as they were acknowledged to be real,
Stevens' aestheticism—which was in fact nothing more than "Art
for Art's sake" carried to its furthest extreme—would be divested
of meaning, just as religion had been invalidated.

Stevens had come to this pass because he lost sight, early in
his career—because of the psychic necessity to survive the loss
of his religion, and because of his subsequent intellectual self-
dazzlement—of something the finest poets have usually under-
stood: poetry is art for man's sake. If Stevens' later austerity is in
fact sterility, what must it have been like to be the only inhabitant
of a mind that existed only for its own existence, at that point
when the mind began to doubt the validity of its existence? Many
have borne the loss of religion, and some have rejoiced in the loss
of the loss of religion, as Stevens did in his early poems. But what
would it be to endure the loss of the loss of the loss of religion?

Many critics, including Waggoner, have remarked on the de-
cline in quality of Stevens' later poems. In the early poems Stevens
was doing what good poets always do: molding language. Even if
one didn't know quite what Stevens was saying because the con-
cepts behind the metaphors were personal and undefined, at least
the metaphors themselves were beautiful, and one could simply
delight in the language as it flowed, like music, over the senses.
When Stevens' concepts began to overbalance the language, when
theory began to become more important than craft, then Stevens
was no longer a poet, he was a philosopher in verse, than which no
creature in any kind of order or disorder is more boring. Waggoner
says:

Unlike Stevens, Aiken does not develop toward more and more abstract
forms of writing. The opposite, rather, is true, as he discovers, in the late

work, the "intelligible forms" implicit in experience, the various melodies
in the chaos. *Sheepfold Hill* (1958) is the work of a poet of advanced age,
but the poems in it are no less sensuous in their texture, and more con-
crete in their approach to people and their experience in time, than the
earliest poem Aiken has cared to preserve. In his late work, Aiken is much
closer to the late Eliot than he is to Stevens. But he no longer *sounds*
like Eliot, as he did so often, and so strikingly, in the early work. Now
he *thinks* like him, and often *feels* like him. The two began at the same
point and developed by utterly different routes to final positions curiously
similar. (*American Poets*, p. 478.)

Aiken may have lost his religion, as Stevens did (and as Eliot did
essentially), but he never ceased to mourn its loss, and he never
forgot that people are real beings, not disembodied intellectual
hermits. If Aiken used poetry to help himself endure, he wanted
his poetry to help others to endure as well. Stevens wanted his
ideas to help himself endure, and the late poetry was, in large part,
merely the vehicle for these ideas. But the folk do not live by ideas
alone; they live in a physical world as well, and Aiken knew how
to build true worlds out of the material of language.

Stevens, from the start, was on a dead-end road, for his theory
was that people must not be romantic about anything, including
the invention of theologies which are, he was sure, based on the
romantic premise that transcendental Beings control man's world
and impose order upon it. Man must stand alone and naked in the
midst of chaos and, by an effort of will, impose the order. But even
this did not go far enough—each man or woman must confront
existence and create his or her own order. Stevens proposed to do
this for himself by using as his framework a theory of language
aesthetics which would stand in the place of the lost theology. If
readers found value in the poems he wrote for himself, that value
was simply a by-product of the act of writing, the real purpose of
which was personal survival in an indifferent world.

Aiken did not find himself in this cul-de-sac, as Waggoner rec-
ognized; rather, the opposite is true: Aiken was the poet Stevens

would have been had he not been more interested in building survival shelters for the Self rather than art for people.

If the current revival of the long narrative poem is successful, we will look to Aiken as one of the few contemporary masters of the form. Many of the poems in his *Collected Poems 1916–1970* (1970) are longer than short, more narrative than lyric; yet it is difficult to place Aiken definitively in any cage of conception or of genre, for he refused to sound like anyone but himself or to conform to mid-century literary etiquette. That is to say, he derived very little from Pound and Eliot except, now and then, a slightly recognizable *weltschmertz*, and even that isn't certain, for it has been argued that Eliot and Pound derived something of their tone from Aiken.

Conrad Aiken's poetry can be explicit and allusive at the same time; it can contain philosophical insights without obtuseness of diction or abstraction of syntax; it can evoke a scene, create a sonic "image," print a spatial pattern without risking thralldom to traditional form or surrealist metaphor. A long story may be told with great variety of locutions, as in "The Coming Forth by Day of Osiris Jones." Here Aiken employs a sequence of related shorter poems with increasingly sharper viewpoints. The life story of O. Jones is told and retold in fragments by clocks, faces, mirrors, and coin machines; in short, the matter of a life becomes its accuser and judge until there is nothing left but the medical report of a dying old man and a "landscape with figures"—birches, larches, pines, junipers; brooks and crickets; echoes and grass—extended over a hollow time.

Aiken lived through both the Modernist and post-Modernist periods, and he survived the New Critics as well as the old simply by writing his own idiosyncratic work and refusing to engage in the literary scene. He was never in the forefront of the era's imagination, nor was he ever a fad. His *Collected Poems* then, was a major book by a major neglected poet. It contained the lifework of

a man who listened with his inner ear to the nuances of the spirit
and of the marrow. Aiken was not satisfied merely to listen, how-
ever. He worked to find the craft that would enable him to convey
to others what he experienced, and he succeeded in his intention
in larger degree than nearly any other poet of the twentieth
century.

The poetry of Conrad Aiken is a poetry of wholeness: whole
meaning, whole experience, whole saying. From first to last his
ouvre is some of the most sustained and exquisite writing the
tongue can boast. Aiken was a musician of the language, and he
heard things in humanity few others have been able to articulate.

It is not so much that he wrote poems as that all his work is a
single poem ranging over personalities and ways of being which
Aiken obviously lived in his mind and committed to paper so that
his audience may live these strangers and familiars as well. He
built, out of words, a cosmos in which an identifiable and evolving
consciousness resides, and that cosmos is large enough to accom-
modate the reader as well as hosts of characters.

One of the reasons why many critics and scholars have found it
difficult to come to terms with Aiken is that he must be perceived
in toto, not in shards and slices. Though the tenor of his creation
has been apparent for some time, the vehicle was not complete at
the time of his death, as no cosmos is ever completed. Never-
theless, it can be argued that in his *ouvre* Aiken accomplished
what Pound did not manage in his *Cantos*. We can finally perceive
that Aiken was a Pythagoras of words—their depth, height, and
breadth. He was a Magus who listened to a linguistic "music of
the spheres," but, like Stevens, he lived in an existential age which
seemed to deny a Pythagorean mathematical harmony of all
things.

What Aiken did, then, was to create a paradox, a universe that
cannot, but which despite all does exist. The tension of his work
derives from the mind's symmetry opposed to the whirlpool of
doubt, rationality struggling with instability, but it is everyman's

struggle, not the ascetic's, for we can all see ourselves standing in the circle of his horizon. The poetry of Aiken is an Ouroboros of consonance and dissonance, the hermetic worm that devours its own tail in order to exist, and in that metaphysical circle which contains all of Man—his mind and his heart, all men and women—all things are encouraged to be until they are extinguished in the total Being.

The Suspect in Criticism

Emerson said in his essay "The Poet" that "criticism is infested with a cant of materialism which assumes that manual skill and activity is the first merit of all men and disparages, such as say and do not, overlooking the fact that some men, namely poets, are natural sayers, sent into the world to the end of expression, and confounds them with those whose province is action but who quit it to imitate the sayers." If we overlook the fact that Emerson himself is at the moment writing criticism, we are to understand that the true poet is born, not made, and those who invent rules for "saying" are not touched with genius but only with self-infatuation.

"For poetry was all written before time was," Emerson continues, "and whenever we are so finely organized that we can penetrate into that region where the air is music, we hear those primal warblings and attempt to write them down, but we lose ever and anon a word or a verse and substitute something of our own, and thus miswrite the poem." The poet, then, is merely an instrument of the Oversoul, a sometimes imperfect instrument. The more finely tuned that instrument, the better the fidelity of his (not her) recording: "The men of more delicate ear write down these cadences more faithfully, and these transcripts, though imperfect, become the songs of the nations." Julian Jaynes would say perhaps that the left hemisphere of the bicameral mind is listening to the right hemisphere, not to the music of the spheres.

Later Emerson writes, "Let us, with new hope, observe how nature . . . has insured the poet's fidelity to his office of announcement and affirming . . . by the beauty of things, which becomes a new and higher beauty when expressed. Nature offers all her creatures to him as a picture-language." We see that Frost was right— Emerson has limited the function of the poet to the expression of the "beautiful." If other things exist, they are not to be given tongue.

Poetry is essential, Emerson feels, for it is merely the expression of what may be sensed all about us, in the universe. The paradox is that "the people fancy they hate poetry, and they are all poets and mystics!" But doesn't that explain why they hate the beautiful as it is written down? Because writing is at a remove from direct experience. Emerson's assertion that this experience "becomes a new and higher beauty when expressed" has a hollow ring to it—what is the purpose of writing it down except to make the universal beauty *conscious*? Direct perception of the "beautiful" is surely better than reading about it in a book.

"Language is fossil poetry," Emerson says, in a wonderful image. But he goes on to undermine it by an inept extension of the metaphor: "As the limestone of the continent consists of infinite masses of the shells of animalcules, so language is made up of images or tropes [he ought to have said *words*], which now, in their secondary use, have long ceased to remind us of their poetic origin. But the poet names the thing because he sees it, or comes one step nearer to it than any other. This expression or naming is not art"—*not* art—"but a second nature, grown out of the first, as a leaf out of a tree." And the theory of "organic poetry" was given its first expression.

This expression has been renewed and restated on any number of occasions during the past century; several of its more recent manifestations appear in the *New Naked Poetry*, edited by Berg and Mezey, which was a second installment of *The Naked Poetry*, published in 1969. In the foreword to the first volume the editors said, "We feel like intruders here. Two years ago, when we first decided that there was a need for a book like this, we planned to start it off with a long essay on the theory and practice of . . . of what? There wasn't even a satisfactory name for the kinds of poetry we were gathering and talking about, and still isn't. Some people said 'Free verse' and others said 'Organic Poetry' (and a few old ones said, 'That's not poetry!'), and we finally came up with Open Forms, which isn't bad but isn't all that good either."

In the second volume the contributors were asked to make their donations to the poetics of organic form or "open poetry," and Kenneth Patchen made a metaphor in order to explain his own approach to the process of creation. "A note on structure: so much nonsense has been written about 'structure' of late (usually by schoolmaster-poets), that a great many people have forgotten that the way to build a house is to build it. Those who work with their hands know that the proper method for moving a heavy stone is to get a good firm hold, brace your feet, kick it into motion with the nubs of your fists, and ride it to where you want it to go."

If anything is clear from Patchen's note, it is that, though he was supposed to be the contemporary workingman's poet, he had no experience in building a house or moving stones. The way *not* to build a house is exactly as Patchen directs; his advice regarding stone-moving will get one sore knuckles and a hernia.

Allen Ginsberg vented some comments on the poetics of "Howl": "Part one uses repeated base who, as a sort of kithera BLANG, homeric (in my imagination) to work off each statement, with rhythmic unit." Perhaps another poet or the reader will have as much trouble digesting this information as in carrying out the Patchen recommendations.

Elsewhere in these pages we have been introduced to the comments of Frank O'Hara, Kenneth Rexroth, and John Logan, and to the tonic words of Galway Kinnell, but here is Charles Simic: "Bashō said: 'a poet does not make a poem—something in him naturally becomes a poem.'" This is a much more intelligible restatement of the Emerson position, but Simic spoils it by going on to make a metaphor: "It's a labor of monks, an order that prays to life on earth. What is a poem if it doesn't equal a bowl of hot soup on a cold winter day?" And Gary Snyder reveals his vision:

> Kiss the ass of the devil and eat shit;
> fuck his horny barbed cock,
> fuck the hag
> and all the celestial angels
> and handmaidens perfum'd and golden—

Perhaps Snyder has a bone to pick with Emerson over the purposes of poetry.

Another contributor to both volumes was William Stafford, who has been vocal over the years regarding his approaches both to writing poetry and to teaching poetry writing. An interview he videotaped in the Writer's Forum series at the State University of New York at Brockport is of particular interest.* Stafford said there that he viewed the act of writing as "a simple encounter with the language," and that this encounter, "if followed with trust, may lead into larger patterns of thought."

"All I want to plead for here," he said later, "is the possibility that around us, if we follow our tentative impulses outward, we may blunder upon one of those reverberating patterns." Writing is largely a matter of overcoming inhibitions, "and if I can 'unlearn' my inhibitions and follow out the impulses that just happen to come to me, I may be led a little way towards some pattern that

---

*A transcript of this tape was published as "Keeping the Lines Wet" in the Summer 1977 issue of *Prairie Schooner*.

reverberates." This is a clear description of the operation of intuition in the creative process.

Stafford is interested in "patterns," but these are not manmade structures of any kind. Rather, they are patterns of experience or of existence. Stafford, however, disavowed any transcendental or mystical pattern, for when he was queried he replied, "I like to agree with anything that sounds as honorific as the words 'spirit' and 'mystical' do to me. I would accept anything that can be found in my writing. But actually I feel that I would like to be as clear and unambiguous as possible in my work. For example, it's precisely for this reason that I feel some reluctance every time I have to use a simile or metaphor. Wouldn't it be better, if we could find the language that would be just exactly right for the poem, without resorting to the 'shimmer of attention' that might cause something important to get away?"

Emerson was not afraid to make a metaphor and catch a pre-historic fish, even though it got away, but Stafford is, if anything, more logical: fancy language gets in the way of the epiphany. Tropes are something to be distrusted. Writing ought to be democratic; Stafford's feeling was that "every person I've ever met who could talk, could write. Writing is just paying attention to what occurs to you; what occurs to everybody. Reluctant as I am to use a comparison, it's like fishing—the person who keeps the line wet catches a fish. A writer is just that person who keeps the line wet, who waits for those little 'nudges' that do come along now and then to all of us." The writer, then, is one who keeps fishing; eventually, after many nibbles, he will catch something—all that's necessary is patience.

"In that case," he was asked—on the premise that one ought to be as good late as early—"do you like your earliest poems as well as you like your latest poems?"

"I thought of a rejoinder for this some time ago," Stafford replied. "To paraphrase Will Rogers: I never met a poem of mine I didn't like." Later he added, "I feel reluctant somehow to learn a technique of poetry without having to. There is a different progression that I would rather follow; maybe it is an organic development."

Stafford was restating Emerson's dictum that "the thought and the form are equal in the order of time, but in the order of genesis the thought is prior to form." Stafford's plainer statement had the advantage that it did not sound like doubletalk. In order to write a poem the poet need only keep his line wet and follow intuitively where the language leads into a pattern of thought, and at that point the thought will choose its own syntax, its own form.

This is a theory so down-to-earth and American that it is un-democratic to suggest that *every* poem must be organic, but that doesn't necessarily mean that one line grows directly out of the line before. Lines grow both ways. A sonnet and an "organic" poem both grow out of the mind and imagination of the author, and they become whatever he is.

If Stafford found it impossible, given his live-and-let-live position, to criticize his own work or to distinguish between his good and better poems, it was equally hard for him to apply critical standards to the work of his students. Alberta Turner, in the "Introduction" to her book *Poets Teaching: The Creative Process* (1980) writes, "Stafford says that his first impulse is 'to become steadfastly evasive until some signal from the student indicates a direction where the student is ready to go.' His method is wholly inductive: 'the first move is the student's move, not mine. . . . If I charge into the poem, I might either take it over or alienate the writer; . . . and I might enhance rather than decrease the dominance implied by teacher-student conferring. Surely our direction is to be toward the writer's taking over of the writing.' He never reaches the stage of overt judgment: 'This succeeds, this fails, this is what you really mean.'"

Another Emersonian poet-critic—identified as such by Waggoner—was less reluctant to codify some of these principles. In 1964 James Dickey published *The Suspect in Poetry*; in it he set up these criteria:

"There are four or five main ways of reacting to poems, and they all matter." Why, then, was the critic unsure of how many ways there are of "reacting"? There was more uncertainty to come:

In ascending order of importance they are (a) "This probably isn't so, and even if it were I couldn't care less," (b) "This may be true enough as far as it goes, but, well . . . so what?" (c) "This is true, or at least convincing, and therefore I respond to it differently than I do to poems in the first two categories," and (d) "This is true with a kind of truth at which I could never have arrived by myself, but its truth is better than the one I believed."

Dickey elaborated these critical categories, and four years later, having once experienced the revelation and found it not wanting, in his book of reprinted reviews *Babel to Byzantium* he wrote a preface that dismissed systematic criticism and logical systems— using the words "intuitive," "mysterious," and "subliminal" to de- scribe his aesthetics—and moved the whole thing from its original place deep in the pages of *The Suspect* to first place in the new work.

In *American Poets*, Waggoner said that Dickey currently "is re- stating in contemporary language some of Emerson's leading ideas about poetry." The unity of Dickey's *Suspect*, Waggoner con- tinued, "springs from Dickey's conviction that poems that seem to lack personal passion and personal vision, poems that resemble autonomous verbal engines, artifacts cleverly designed to stir our emotions without giving us any new perception, any 'fresh glimpse of the world,' are 'suspect.' We do and should resist them, Dickey argues, since we do not want to be manipulated by poets any more than by advertisers."

In the war between Emersonian mysticism and the New Criti- cism's dominance, at that time, of American literary theory,

Waggoner was not a neutral. "The surprising, the 'radical' thing" about Dickey's criticism, he said,

> is the poet's unabashed use of "truth" where the modern masters have taught us to expect "myth" or "fictive music." Reading Dickey's words we might almost imagine we were listening to Frost in his old age, when his guard was down, talking about what he really cared about in poetry and hoped the young men [*sic*.] would care about. As for the reference to the poet's "vision" . . . , talk about "vision" has been taboo among poets, and even more among critics, since Pound omitted it from his requirements for good poetry.
>
> But of course "vision" as Dickey uses it here stops short of being fully Emersonian, or transcendental and religious, in its implication.

This was the crux of the problem in Dickey's work, both in his poetry and in his criticism, just as it is the problem of anyone who wants to bypass craft and get right down to the nitty-gritty of mystical experience, for Dickey straddled a chasm and seemed incapable of bringing his feet together either on one side of the gulf or on the other. Even further beyond his capacity, judging from the later *Babel*, is what he would have liked to do: bring the two faces of the chasm together in a fusion of vision and art. It is the problem of our time, and of any other, as perhaps even Waggoner would admit, for when he criticized a poet it was as often for a lack of craft as for a lack of insight. But if there was a certain sense of ambivalence, of split-mindedness in some of Waggoner's judgments, this sense was even more acute in Dickey's. Dickey had an aversion to rhymed poetry, for instance. In the essay titled "The Poet Turns on Himself," he said:

> I had in the beginning a strong dislike of rhyming poems, for the element of artificiality is one of the characteristics of poetry I most distrust, and I have always had trouble distinguishing between artificiality and the traditional modes and methods of verse; for a time I was convinced that craft and artifice were the same thing. At the same time I also had a secret suspicion that Whitman, Lawrence, the Imagists and others were cheating, absolving themselves from the standing problems and difficulties of verse.

Dickey was a victim of the Anglo-American confusion of mode, but his troubles were just beginning:

> But I found, unlike so many others, that the qualities of poems which seemed to me poetic—*essentially* poetic—were not in the least dependent on whether or not they occurred in poems which were rhymed. I also discovered that the restrictions imposed by rhyme led me away from what I had intended to say.

Having been defeated by the exigencies of rhyme, Dickey had to consider what other element of craft he would jettison. Would it be meter? Not quite:

> Although I didn't care for rhyme and the "packaged" quality which it gives even the best poems, I did care very much for meter, or at least rhythm. . . . Most of the material I read on metrics concluded that the systematic use of anapests and dactyls tends to monotony, and I accepted this judgment on faith and continued to try to work with the customary English iambic line.

But the iamb would work no better for Dickey than would rhyme. Fortunately, however, he "found that the anapest was as capable of interesting variation as any other kind of line; in fact, as the iamb itself." He found, further, that what he "really wanted to do was to make effective *statements*." So he began, in his earlier work—the poems that appeared in *Into the Stone* (1960)—to use anapests, dactyls, and "a kind of refrain technique that, so far as I know, I invented for the occasion. In this, the last or refrain lines of the stanzas unite to make, themselves, a last stanza which sums up the attitude and action of the poem."

Dickey, setting out to reinvent poetry, had not, evidently, discovered that his invention is at least as old as the medieval Provençal verse forms (such as the villanelle and the triolet with which Robinson, Roethke, Thomas and others had been recently working) that do the same thing, though they rhyme as well. In his later book, *Self-Interviews* (1970) Dickey seems to be saying something quite different: "While I was writing *Into the Stone*, I was very much interested in experimenting with verse forms. I've always been a great admirer of Hardy and tried to take a lesson from him in inventing. He seemed to get a good deal of enjoyment from inventing forms." And it was from Hardy's *Collected Poems*, Dickey now recalls, that he got the idea for his "summation or coda" stanzas.

One might well be wondering at the amount of time an Emersonian was spending worrying about craft. In *Babel* Dickey wrote further that he "discovered that the simple declarative sentence, under certain circumstances and in certain contexts, had exactly the qualities I wanted my lines of poetry to have. As I wrote more poems of this kind, I was increasingly aware of two things. The first was that I liked poems which had a basis of narrative." Thus, the visionary added two more techniques to his store—grammatics and narrative, and yet a third, stream-of-consciousness, though Dickey didn't use the term:

I also discovered that I worked most fruitfully in cases in which there was no clearcut distinction between what was actually happening and what was happening in the mind of a character in the poem. I meant to try to get a fusion of inner and outer states, of dream, fantasy, and of illusion where everything partakes of the protagonist's mental processes and creates a single impression.

Many of the terms he was using at that point were from the discipline of fiction: "character," "illusion," "protagonist," and with all of these things, there was the technical fusion at last:

My second book, *Drowning with Others*, is made up of poems written in this manner: poems with a predominantly anapestic rhythm and dealing often with dream, hallucination, fantasy, the interaction of illusion and reality. My third book, *Helmets*, employed many of these same themes and approaches, but was less pronouncedly rhythmical and less hallucinatory. By this time I had begun to grow a little restive at the limitations of my method and was beginning also to dislike the way I had been handling the narrative elements. All my old reservations about the vitiating effects of artifice began to trouble me once more; I was afraid that I had simply substituted another set of conventions—or artifices—for those I had congratulated myself on discarding earlier.

Perhaps we, too, are growing too restive to follow the poet through his reinvention of English-language poetry leading eventually to what he calls "the 'open' poem." In short, Dickey wanted very much to be a member of what Waggoner called "the Emersonian mainstream." Language is to be used only as an instrument of "vision," of "insight" and "revelation," not for "literary" purposes; language is not to be tolerated as an element, in and of itself, of American poetry. There is, in fact, to be no such thing as "literature" at all, only "higher consciousness."

Yet the word would intrude, artifice kept getting in the way, and Dickey now and then stumbled over it, as in this passage from the essay in *Babel* on Hayden Carruth:

"On a Certain Engagement South of Seoul" is as fine a poem as an American has ever written about the ex-soldier's feelings, and that takes in a lot of territory. It is only after the Inevitable has clamped us by the back of the neck that we go back and look carefully at the poem, and see that it is written in *terza rima.* And so, hushed and awed, we learn something about the power of poetic form, and the way in which it can both concentrate and release meaning, when meaning is present.

The poets who argue for "open form" in poetry, however reluctantly, nevertheless make a simile—like Emerson, like Stafford—to carry their argument. A poem, they say, should not be arbitrarily restricted by some preconceived convention such as meter or stanza pattern, which will inhibit free expression. Rather, the poem ought to grow the way a plant does, putting down a root here, "intuitively," between these grains of loam, seeking the water that wells up from the living rock; putting forth a leaf there, to catch that slant of morning sun.

Not content with one figure of speech, the organic poets extend the simile until it has blossomed into full-blown metaphor, and then into a conceit: the word "like" is abandoned and the stronger "is" is substituted—the poem is a tree of words: take a cross-section of the trunk and read in the rings there the hard seasons and the lean. Or the poem is a conch, each whorl telling its tale of growth and search.

Say it were true—the poem is a plant, an organism of langauge. Take a particular poem, or a particular plant. What kind of plant is it? What kind of poem? Is it a crocus, such as Muriel Rukeyser mentions in her essay in *The New Naked Poetry*? Is it pennyroyal, is it rue or sage? The plant itself may not know its name as we do, but it "knows" what it is. Plant an acorn, and a maple will not grow. The tree will be restricted in its general form to the pattern implanted in its genes and chromosomes. The individual tree will differ in detail, but not in substance, from each of its fellows of the genus; it will be an oak with oak leaves and oak roots, oak bark and oaken form. It will produce acorns, not maple wings.

Then what sort of poem is a "free form" poem? Is it a mapleoak or a crocusfrog? Is it Rappaccini's garden of unearthly delights? Is it a sterile mule? Or is it perhaps a stream, seeking the path of least resistance from the mountain spring to the tidal plain? What kinds of tropes are these to which Emerson and his poets have "given birth" in order to justify their practice? What kind of poem is it that seeks the path of least resistance?

Black Poetry

In his long scholarly introduction to the anthology *Understanding the New Black Poetry* (1973), Stephen Henderson goes deeply into "Black techniques." Henderson believes that large questions about the value of Black poetry "cannot be resolved without considering the ethnic roots of Black poetry, which . . . are ultimately understood only by Black people themselves."

As long as it is "ethnic roots" we're talking about, we might go farther: a poem may be so heavily ethnic that most who do not belong to the group could not understand, let alone judge, such a poem. "Language is the main cohesive force within a given ethnic group," as Arthur Koestler has pointed out, "but, at the same time, it creates barriers and acts as a repellent force between groups." It is quite possible for Black writers to use English in such ways as to speak directly to a Black audience while, at the same time, the white audience is held at bay. This is done by manipulation of techniques and development of Black styles, however, not by using particular techniques labeled "Black" as distinguished from others labeled "White." The language techniques used in such poems would be analyzable, and those same techniques would appear in many other kinds of poetry.

Henderson says:

> Although it is an arbitrary scheme for the purpose of analysis, one may describe or discuss a "Black" poem in terms of the following broad categories: (1) Theme, (2) Structure, (3) Saturation.
>
> (1) By *theme* I mean that which is being spoken of, whether the specific subject matter, the emotional response to it, or its intellectual formulation.
>
> (2) By *structure* I mean chiefly some aspect of the poem such as diction, rhythm, figurative language, which goes into the total makeup. (At times, I use the word in an extended sense to include what is usually called genre.)
>
> (3) By *saturation* I mean several things, chiefly the communication of "Blackness" and fidelity to the observed or intuited truth of the Black Experience in the United States. It follows that these categories should also be valid in any critical evaluation of the poem.

One need not quarrel much with the first and third of these categories except to point out that "emotional response" has more to do with the sensory level of a poem than with its ideational level; nor need one object to the parenthetical material in Henderson's second category. There are obviously many specifically Black themes possible, but writers of other ethnic groups could, if they wished, write on these themes as well, and many have done so. Certainly, there are genres, or kinds of Black writing, some of which we will discuss here. With regard to "saturation"—it is equally evident that poetry can be heavily saturated with Black ethnic referents. One must, however, call into question many of Henderson's remarks about Black techniques under his heading of "Structure." The first of these is:

A. "Virtuoso naming and enumerating." Though Henderson doesn't say so in so many words, he implies that this is a specifically Black technique, the roots of which "might conceivably lie in the folk practice of riddling and similar kinds of wordplay." As an example, Henderson recommends Ted Joans' "The Nice Colored Man," a portion of which reads,

Nice Nigger Educated Nigger Never Nigger Southern Nigger Clever Nigger Northern Nigger Nasty Nigger Unforgiveable Nigger Unforgettable Nigger Unspeakable Nigger Rude & Uncouth Nigger Mean & Vicious Nigger Smart Black Nigger Smart Black Nigger Smart Black Nigger Smart Black Nigger Smart Black Nigger . . .

Henderson is right in his derivation of this tradition from folk literature, but not in his implication that the folk are Black in particular. Here is #749 from the Baring-Goulds' *The Annotated Mother Goose*:

> There was a man, and his name was Dob,
> And he had a wife, and her name was Mob,
> And he had a dog, and he called it Cob,
> And she had a cat, called Chitterabob,
>   Cob, says Dob,
> Chitterabob, says Mob,
> Cob was Dob's dog
> Chitterabob Mob's cat.

This nursery rhyme, however, is of later derivation than the sixteenth-century English poet John Skelton's "Ware the Hawk," a portion of which reads,

> Of no tyrant I read
> That so far did exceed,
> Neither Diocletian,
> Nor yet Domitian,
> Nor yet crooked Cacus,
> Nor yet drunken Bacchus;
> Neither Olibrius,
> Nor Dionysius,
> Neither Phalary
> Rehearsed in Valery;
> Nor Sardanapall . . . ,

and so on. One might cite other examples, including Whitman. The standard term for this technique is "cataloguing," and it is in this particular poem of Joans' also a form of repetition, particularly incremental repetition.

B. "Jazzy rhythmic effects." Henderson is vague about this technique. He says, "Compare these lines from LeRoi Jones' 'T. T. Jackson Sings' with the traditional dozens lines which are printed just below them."

> I fucked your mother
> On top of a house
> When I got through
> She thought she was
> Mickey Mouse
>   *   *   *   *
> I fucked your mother from house to house
> Out came a baby named Minnie Mouse.

Both verses are written in the prosody called "dipodics," which is a derivation from Anglo-Saxon (accentual) prosody. It is notably the "folk" prosody of nursery rhymes, ballads, and riddles—both the nursery rhyme and the Skelton piece quoted earlier are dipodic. Here is a verse whose rhythms are very close to those of the first example:

> There was an old woman
> Who lived in a shoe.
> She had so many children,
> She didn't know what to do.

Henderson's other examples are very different, mostly prose poems, some of them rhymed. It's difficult to see what these various techniques have in common; they go by different names in prosodic terminology. There is, though, a *tradition* of scatological humorous podic verse in the Black community called "dozens," as Henderson points out. This tradition is identifiably ethnic in content and in style, though not in technique. Poe's "The Bells" has been discussed in the twentieth century as a "jazz poem" written before jazz had been invented, and here is a poem written in 1959 before one knew that whites were not supposed to do this sort of thing: *

Lorrie

Lorrie looked good: man,
    she was a jazz band, straight
    as a clarinet, and the tunes she played
    with her hip action wowed my crowd.
Lorrie swung like a good ensemble,
    smiled the cool blues as we sipped our
    brews in the racetrack dive while the
    bass thrummer, a basic type, swiped
    at the strings, making us think
    of beds and things.
There we were, dancing our eyes
    among the beers while Lorrie walked
    her gay way among us, mashers all,
    and we asked, "What's up tonight,
    Lorrie-love?"
"I've no time," she smiled, "no time—
    I'm a college lass, my major's law.
"By night I slide drinks down
    to your hands, and in the daylight
    I guard lives at Ryall's Beach."
Then, when the jazz bunch quit and
    the horn stopped snorting
    and the drums bumped the last bum
    out the door, we went too, man,
    we went too.

Who wants to see Lorrie meet her beau;
    who wants to see his old eyes, older
    than she'll ever be, and his dark hands
    grab her wrist hard as they leave to park
    in the raceway woods?

---

* From my chapbook *The Sketcher* (1962); reprinted in *Pocoangelini: A Fantography, and Other Poems* (1971).

Henderson mentions "blues" as a quality of jazz in the poems he cites. Perhaps we can put off till later the question of Black musical *forms* as bases for Black "techniques."

C. "Virtuoso free-rhyming." Henderson says in effect that these examples typify a Black tradition:

> I don't want nothin old but some gold;
> I don't want nothin black but a Cadillac!
>
> I can't eat a bite, I can't sleep at night,
> Cause the woman I love don't treat me right.
>
> They call me Rap the dicker the ass kicker
> The cherry picker and city slicker the titty licker . . . (Anonymous)

There may be in these fragments identifiably Black "themes" and "saturations," but no race or ethnic group has a corner on the "free rhyming" or internal rhyme markets—nor, for that matter, on scatology. Here is Skelton again, in "The Tunning of Elinor Rumming":

> With a whim-wham
> Knit with a trim-tram
> Upon her brain-pan
> Like an Egyptian . . .
>
>   *   *   *   *
>
> But let us turn plain,
> There we left again.
> For as ill a patch as that,
> The hens run in the mash-vat;
> For they go to roost
> Straight over the ale-joust,
> And dung, when it comes,
> In the ale-tunnes.

And here is another nursery rhyme, #751:

> I need not your needles, they're needless to me,
> For kneading of needles is needless, you see,
> But did my neat trousers but need to be kneed,
> I then should have need of your needles indeed.

Finally, here's a piece from Robert Burns' "The Kirk's Alarm":

> Dr. Mac, Dr. Mac, you should stretch on a rack,
>   To strike evil-doers wi' terror;
> To join faith and sense upon onie pretence,
>   Is heretic, damnable error.

Burns' poem is, indeed, ethnic, but ethnic Scots.

D. "Hyperbolic imagery." Henderson says, "The breathless virtuoso quality of free-rhyming comes from the utilization of a single rhyme sound, the object being to get in as many rhymes as one can." Though he doesn't intend it, Henderson's is about as good a definition of Skelton's dipodic method as one could wish, a method called after its inventor, *Skeltonics*, or "tumbling verse." "Oratorically," Henderson continues, "this is balanced by a passage in which there is no rhyme at all, and the wit and the energy expend themselves in a series of hyperbolic wisecracks, rooted in the tradition of masculine boasting." He gives an example from the folk tradition:

> I'm the man who walked the water and tied the whale's tail in a knot
> Taught the little fishes how to swim
> Crossed the burning sands and shook the Devil's hand
> Rode round the world on the back of a snail carrying a sack saying
>   AIR MAIL.

There's nothing new about the "brag"—medieval British poets understood it as a basic convention. It should go without saying that "hyperbole" is an ancient Greek term, and this type of stylized American hyperbole is called "the backwoods boast" by folklorists. It was a feature of the westward movement of the nineteenth century.

E. "Metaphysical imagery." In speaking of this category Henderson mentions its uses in English literature. He does not, evidently, mean to make a case for this technique's being particularly "Black."

F. Henderson polishes off "understatement" in four lines without making racial claims for it.

G. "Compressed and cryptic imagery." Henderson here is as cryptic as his subheading. The example he gives is a brag from Ellison's *Invisible Man*. No definition is offered beyond "arcane references to what I have called 'mascon' imagery." We will discuss "masconception" later; meanwhile, Henderson makes no claims that Black poets can be more obscure than other kinds of poets.

H. "Worrying the line." Henderson says, "This is the folk expression for the device of altering the pitch of a note in a given passage or for other kinds of ornamentation often associated with melismatic singing in the Black tradition. A verbal parallel exists in which a word or phrase is broken in order to allow for affective or didactic comment. Here is an example from Rich Amerson's 'Black Woman'":

> Say, I feel superstitious, Mama
> 'Bout my hoggin' bread, Lord help my hungry time,
> I feel superstitious, Baby, 'bout my hoggin' bread!
> Ah-hmmmm, Baby, I feel superstitious,
> I say 'stitious, Black Woman!
> Ah-hmmmm, ah you hear my cryin'
> About I done got hungry, oh Lordy!
> Oh, Mama, I feel superstitious
> About my hog Lord God it's my bread.

"Melismatic" means, according to the *O.E.D.*, "the art of florid or ornate vocalization." Henderson makes much, later on, of musical comparisons between Black poetry and Black music. The language techniques illustrated by the Amerson passage Henderson quotes are such things as parallelism, incremental repetition, orthographical schemas—elision and apocopation primarily. That Amerson's poem is written in a Black style and tradition is not open to question, but one can find hundreds of examples of the same techniques in English poetry of all periods.

At this point in his essay Henderson defines his neologism "mascon": "a massive concentration of Black experiential energy." If we look at the poem by Amerson just cited, we see that it is clearly a Black poem, but it is not the techniques that make them Black, it is how the techniques are applied. There is "mascon" in the poems, but the "massive concentration of Black experiential energy" is a function of style, not structure.

No one could have faulted Henderson if he had called the second of his three major critical categories "Style" rather than "Structure," or, better, "Styles"—there is more than one Black style of writing, as Henderson recognizes, but his insisting on identifying particular English language techniques as being somehow "Black" confuses the issue, as for instance when he speaks about "the Black oratorical technique of repetition." This, as we have mentioned in an earlier chapter, is the oldest prosody in the world, and it is universal; we call it grammatic parallelism, and it includes the device of repetition. It is to be found in prose poetry as well as in verse poetry—the Bible is full of it, and Henderson gives an example from Martin Luther King's "I Have a Dream" speech. Where does Henderson imagine that the Rev. Dr. King got his oratorical style if not from the Bible? That King's adaptation of this prosodic system gives rise to an identifiably Black traditional style is also apparent.

Included in the section on "Structure" in Henderson's essay is a subsection titled "Black Music as Poetic Reference." Henderson says, "Aside from mascon structure, there are other important ways in which music, Black music, lies at the basis of much Black poetry, either consciously or covertly. I have been able to distinguish at least ten types of usage."

That poetry and music have always been closely associated in all traditions is a truism. Here Henderson is speaking about Black music and poetry:

In No. 1, "*the casual, generalized reference*, there are mere suggestions of Black song types." In Henderson's examples there are mentions of "everlasting song," "Caroling softly souls of slavery," "Blues," "jazz," "slave songs," "jubilees" and more generalized musical references. He makes no claim that general reference is a particularly Black technique.

"In No. 2, there is a careful allusion to song titles." "For a reader familiar with these songs, the titles evoke a more particularized response, and the effect thus borders on the 'subjective correlative' alluded to in type seven." By this term Henderson evidently means an emotional response triggered by, in this case, a Black song title. Particular songs and singers carry loads of cultural and ethnic associations and overtones for American Blacks. Plainly, though, the technique of allusion is not racial. We will discuss the so-called "subjective correlative" when we come to item No. 7.

In No. 3, "*Quotations from a song* are incorporated into the poem." The comments regarding "No. 2," above, apply.

No. 4 is "Adaptations of song forms," which "include blues, ballads, hymns, children's songs, work songs, spirituals, and popular songs." Henderson says that in particular the ballad, the hymn, and the blues are "numerous and easily recognizable." He continues, "The first two have numerous parallels in other literary traditions. But the blues as a literary form was developed and refined by Langston Hughes and later by Sterling Brown, though Hughes clearly overstated his case for the fixity of the blues form in his preface to *Fine Clothes for the Jew*."

There is a difference between "technique" and "form." Techniques are universal within a language—often, just plain universal—but specific forms may develop in any culture or social heritage. We may grant Henderson his claim that the blues and jazz are specifically Black American *forms*, perhaps, although Browning's "A Toccata of Galuppi's" looks very bluesy in form. Henderson mentions the "'classic' twelve-bar, three line form" of the blues, as in Eddie "Son" House's "Dry Spell Blues":

The dry spell blues have fallen, drove me from door to door.
Dry spell blues have fallen, drove me from door to door.
The dry spell blues have put everybody on the killing floor.

Now the people down south sure won't have no home.
Now the people down south sure won't have no home.
'Cause the dry spell have parched all this cotton and corn.

And so forth. Here is a portion of the Browning poem:

Here you come with your old music, and here's all the good it brings.
What, they lived once thus at Venice where the merchants were the
      kings,
Where Saint Mark's is, where the Doges used to wed the sea with rings.

The rhythms and rhymes are the same. The only thing missing from the Browning poem is the formal repetition. The main point is that, though the *forms* differ slightly, the *techniques* are the same. The *styles* are completely different.

"Device No. 5 is the practice, with considerable variety, of *forcing the reader to incorporate into the structure of the poem his memory of a specific song or passage of a song, or even of a specific delivery technique.* Without this specific memory the poem cannot be properly realized." Evidently, this particular Black "technique" depends heavily either on a shared life experience, or on the reader's having a phonograph record of a particular Black musician.

Henderson expends a good deal of energy in elaborating this "device" of "arcane" allusion (the quoted words are his), ranging from Percy Johnston's "Number Five Cooper Square"—

> I remember Clifford tossing
> Bubbles, Scit! Whoom!, from an
> Ante-bellum moon. Scit! And
> Killer Joe's golden chain, Scit!
> While Ornette gives a lecture on
> A Sanscrit theme with Bachian
> Footnotes, scit. . . . [*Bach*ian?]

—to "Don Lee's famous poem 'Don't Cry, Scream'" which contains "the stylized [*n.b.*] *visual* representation . . . 'sing/loud &/ high/with/feeling' and 'sing/loud &/long/with feeling'" to "the stylized rendition of the Coltrane sound"—

> I can see my me, it was truth you gave,
> like a daily shit
> it had to come.
>
>   can you scream------brother? very
>   can you scream------brother? soft
>
> I hear you.
> I hear you.
>
> and the Gods will too.

The twentieth-century British poet Dame Edith Sitwell had done similar things in "Polka" from *Façade*:

> '. . . As they watch me dance the polka,'
> Said Mr. Wagg like a bear,
> 'In my top hat and my whiskers that—
> Tra la la la, trap the Fair.
>
> Tra la la la la
> Tra la la la la—
> Tr la la la la la la la
>   La
>   La!'

Henderson speaks about references to Black music forms, performers, and performances, but one can use this technique to refer to any sort of music that may be familiar to an audience, as W. S. Gilbert did in *H.M.S. Pinafore*:

> When the foeman bares his steel,
>   Tarantara! tarantara!
> We uncomfortable feel,
>   Tarantara!
> And we find the wisest thing,
>   Tarantara! tarantara

> Is to slap our chests and sing
>> Tarantara!
> For when threatened with emeutes,
>> Tarantara! tarantara!
> And your heart is in your boots,
>> Tarantara!
> There is nothing brings it round.
>> Tarantara! tarantara!
> Like the trumpet's martial sound,
>> Tarantara! tarantara!
> Tarantara-ra-ra-ra-ra!

In the eighteenth century Christopher Smart wrote a prose poem that is practically a treatise on this sort of thing, "Of the Spiritual Musick."

"In the sixth kind of musical referent," Henderson continues, "*precise musical notation is incorporated into the text of the poem.*" This device goes back as far as the invention of musical notation. Certainly, texts have always been written for music and vice-versa. William Walton wrote music for Sitwell's *Façade*, and there is a recording of her reading the poems to his music—not singing them, *reading* them. Thomas Campion published his first *Book of Ayres* in 1601 and a treatise on "Counter-Point" later on. The connection of music with poetry is ancient and continuing— Sidney Lanier, the poet-musician, had a theory of the "symphonic poem" in the nineteenth century, as has been discussed in an earlier chapter.

"In device number seven, the reader's *emotional response to a well-known song is incorporated into the poem* in a manner resembling the use of a 'rest' in music or an assumed 'obbligato.'" Henderson's use of traditional musical terms speaks for itself. This is merely an elaboration of devices nos. 2–5, with the addition that a cue-word or phrase is used as a refrain, as in the example given from Robert Terrell's "'Asian Stew,' with its play on the word 'jelly.'"

Wit rice-n-mud-n-bamboo shoots
Wit sizzled hairs-n-human eclairs
Wit shrapnel-n-goodwill-n-jelly
jelly jelly.

Probably anyone who had lived through the Vietnam War would understand this poem with its double-entendre on the word "jelly."

Henderson says, "Since the reference is to a state of mind or feeling instead of to an object or structure, the technique could be called the use of the 'subjective correlative,' in contrast to the 'objective correlative of the New Criticism."

"Subjective correlative" is an impressive term for "cue" or "cue-word." Such words are intended as automatic triggers for culturally conditioned emotional responses. The technique is no different in kind from the use of the words "apple pie," "motherhood," or "Old Glory" in a political speech. It is not particularly a poetic device, but a rhetorical one. It is, in fact, rather antipoetic in that it requires little skill on the part of the writer—all he needs is to be tapped into the ethos of his audience in order to find the particular word that will set off the response desired. The question, then, is whether the poet will settle for the effect of the word alone or build a context for it that provides the alien reader with points of reference which will allow him to understand some of the overtones with which the cues are laden.

In the eighth of Henderson's "devices," "The musician himself functions as subject, poem, history, or myth." This technique is the same in all cultures: reference to a culture hero of some sort. That in this case the referent is a musician is a very slight reason for the critic's listing it here.

Device No. 9 is "Language from the jazz life or associated with it, commonly called 'hip' speech." There is nothing new about dialect poetry, nor even slang poetry—see the poem "Lorrie" cited earlier here. One cannot think why Henderson lists this "device"; the only reason conceivable seems to be that "hip" talk uses a number of jazz musical terms, and Henderson is intent upon distinguishing jazz, for cultural reasons, from other forms of music. Where does that leave the other Black musical forms he listed earlier, the spirituals and so forth?

Henderson writes, "In the tenth category, *the poem as 'score' or 'chart,'* we move to the most challenging aspect of Black poetic structure—the question of limit, or performance of the text." (It should be noted that he is still saying "structure," not "style" or "tradition.") Later Henderson says, "A poem may thus differ from performance to performance just as jazz performances of 'My Favorite Things' would. Moreover, it implies that there is a Black poetic mechanism, much like the musical ones, which can transform a Shakespearian sonnet into a jazz poem, the basic conceptual model of contemporary Black poetry. The technique, the fundamental device, would be improvisation, lying as it does at the very heart of jazz music."

Neither in music nor in poetry is improvisation in any way linked merely to jazz or to a specific ethnic group. The Arabic *qasida* is a form dating from prehistoric times, and its essence is improvisation. As to turning Shakespearian sonnets into jazz poems, one can even blend the sonnet with the blues; this following sequence, written by Wesli Court, is a set of terza-rima blues sonnets, ending with a pure blues sonnet as an envoi:

> The Boneyard Blues
>
> I.
> I'm sitting in the boneyard singing songs,
> Sitting singing songs as blue as blue—
> Considering my days, their shorts and longs,
>
> The days we spent together, me and you.
> Yes, you and me and all those other folks
> Who've come and gone. Oh, please don't misconstrue
>
> My meaning—yesterday is gone in strokes,
> In strokes and chimes, and time cannot be turned,
> I'm well aware; it plays its dirty jokes

And leaves us on our ashes, bare and burned.
We bare our hearts, and then we burn our spans,
But who's to say what lessons we have learned?

The ifs and maybes, shall-bes, will-bes, cans
Turn into bonedust, rusting pots and pans.

II.
Rusting pots and pans pile up and ring,
Pile up and ring us round with shards of loss,
With echoes of the songs we used to sing

In living rooms and bedrooms filled with moss,
With moss and lichen now of recollection.
The kitchen where we used to sit and toss

Together meals of love and of affection
Has grown a mold upon the oven grate,
And there is nothing left of our confection

Except a little sweeting on a plate,
The plate of dreams, its edges chipped and cracked.
In the beginning already it was too late—

The gun was loaded and the deck was stacked.
The tune could not provide what the lyrics lacked.

III.
And so I'm sitting in this boneyard, blue
As blue, and singing songs that leave me cold.
The words—they may be false, they may be true,

They may be new—more likely they are old,
As old as flesh and time. I hear the knell
Of generations as the peals are rolled

Among the stones, within the stony well—
That stone-cold well of destiny gone dry.
Who is the sexton hauling on the bell?

Why is the deacon grinning at us? Why?
Why are his cheekbones sunken, and his teeth
So moonlight-gleaming? Wherefore is his eye

The hollow of a heartbeat underneath
The zero of a withered floral wreath?

Envoi
Just let me drop this note into the dark,
Yes, let me drop this note into the dark—
I'll light it with a match and watch it spark.

I'll sail it into night with fire and flare,
Fly it into darkness, see it flare
And wink out in those shadows circling there.

I'll watch it take its place among the stars,
Among the minor planets and the stars.
I'll hum the blues, not much—a couple bars—

Until the spark has died to inky ash,
And words have flickered into smoken ash.
Then I'll have me a sip of sour mash,

And lean against this marker made of stone
That will not last as long as ink or bone.

One of the purposes of Henderson's book, evidently, is to provide young Black poets with an arsenal of weapons to use in writing poetry that is acceptably ethnic. But it is important also that young poets understand the differences between "styles" and "techniques." A style is something that develops with skill, experience, and personality; technique, on the other hand, can be studied and learned. To confuse the two things, as Henderson does, is to do a disservice to developing poets by making something racial of some of the tools that all writers have in common.

If young Black poets believe there are "Black" techniques and "white" techniques, it is likely that they will turn away from the conscious development of skills in the language they must use and turn instead to imitations of approved styles already developed and patented by their predecessors and elders. If such a situation develops, the danger exists that there will be a generation of Black writers who are imitators rather than poets. Blake said in the first "Preface" to his *Jerusalem*, "Poetry fettered, fetters the human race. Nations are destroyed or flourish in proportion as their poetry, painting, and music are destroyed or flourish. The primeval state of man was wisdom, art, and science."

Considering Post-Modernism

In the Foreword to his anthology *The Voice That Is Great within Us* (1970), Hayden Carruth writes:

When I was a young poet in the 1940's I felt chronologically deprived, and so did my friends. We had been born too late, that was our trouble. The great epoch of "modern poetry" was in the past; its works, which we desperately admired, *The Waste Land, Lustra, Harmonium, Spring and All* and so many others, had been written long ago and had exhausted the poetic impetus. Nothing was left for us to do. Avidly we sought old magazines in which to experience vicariously the fervor of once-ringing manifestoes and the exciting first appearances of tradition-shattering poems. We sought, too, the old-timers who could regale us with the gossip that never dies. What was it really like in Paris during the 1920's, or in London a decade earlier? These were the issues that seemed to us most interesting.

It must, indeed, have been intimidating to be born into the generation that succeeded the generation of Modernists. By the time these poets were going to college, especially those who matriculated after serving in World War II, not only had the American Poetic Revolution opened everything up, it had also closed down the town. Furthermore, by the 1940's not only was the Revolution

over and expanded to the size of myth, it was being institution-
alized by the academics who were waiting to welcome those vet-
erans who were struggling to become poets themselves—they had
to endure the double burden of myth and institution.

Inasmuch as there seemed to be nowhere left to go, these
younger poets simply continued to write. If vertical achievement
seemed out of the question, at least one might manage something
on the horizontal plane. After a number of years had passed the
Post-Modernist generation could look back and say, as Carruth
did in the same Foreword:

> Now, of course, I have come to understand that my own life has been
> equally blest, my own time equally interesting. Not only were members of
> my generation already beginning, in 1945, to produce works that would
> rival the past, but the old-timers themselves, at least many of them, were
> still looking forward to their best poems; and the quarter-century since
> then has been rich in poetic experience.

The poets of the post-Modernist period were not all alike, by
any means, but certain generalizations can be made about many of
them, given the literary environment in which they found them-
selves. First, many of the Modernists had been experimental and
had deliberately developed idiosyncratic styles. While it was im-
possible not to be influenced by people like cummings, Stevens,
and Moore, it was equally impossible to imitate them or to de-
velop their styles further. Odd styles were, for the most part, out.
A more likely possibility was to be influenced by the style of Eliot;
another was to listen to Eliot's theoretics—as they were being
promulgated by the New Critics—with regard to the classicism
and balance of the best poetry, and to follow the example of Pound
(at least in his early formal poetry), Robinson, and Frost when it
came to questions of craft.

In the aftermath of the Modernist explosion there was among
many poets a return to the American bardic tradition which had
been achieving some very solid poetry for the first time in Ameri-
can history just prior to, and in the early phases of, the Revolu-

tion. Poets like Randall Jarrell, Delmore Schwartz, and the earlier Robert Lowell wrote poems in the Symbolist tradition of Eliot. Anthony Hecht, Richard Wilbur, Howard Nemerov and others turned for models to the English Renaissance and the metaphysical tradition of Donne, whom Eliot had resurrected, and began to write a poetry of elegance. Karl Shapiro did something similar but, dissatisfied and discontented with the lowered sights of his generation, he began to experiment with various techniques and theories till at last he appeared to be a sort of latter-day academic Ezra Pound. Some poets, including Weldon Kees, picked up not only the techniques but the dark song of the pre-Modernists Robinson and Frost, transmuting it into postwar despair.

As Carruth pointed out, during all this time most of the Modernists themselves were still writing and publishing. Williams was active in the periodicals and among the younger poets, sowing the seeds of a neo-Imagism that sprouted in the mid-1960's into "deep image" surrealism that descended "like a pink cloud" (to use a simile of Dugan Gilman) over the campuses, to be picked up through osmosis by an enormous generation of college workshop poets, a cloud from which academe did not begin to emerge until the 1980's. This literary smog colored the self-indulgence that began with "Beat" in the early, and "confessional" poetry in the late 1950's, worked its way through the antiwar and protest poetry of the 1960's, and continues to taint feminist poetry. For this we have not only Whitman to thank, but another male, Robert Lowell, who dropped the formal lyricism of the first "confessional" poet, W. D. Snodgrass, and went straight to writing slack prose poems from his earlier highly-wrought pseudo-Donne pieces.

This was the true post-Modernist revolution: for the first time in United States history, writers were being allowed to teach in college English departments in significant numbers. For whatever reason, there were poets and novelists in the classroom actually interacting with students and, to be sure, teaching the artifacts and precepts of Modernism. If it was not actually coined during the 1940's, at least there began to radiate into our literary vocabulary shortly thereafter the term "academic poet," which was soon to become a pejorative label. The academic revolution soon progressed so far that Paul Engle at the University of Iowa could expand the first program ever specifically designed to provide an education for writers, and the graduates of Iowa spread into the American academic world to teach writing-arts courses and found many another graduate, and even now and then an undergraduate program which, in turn, sent out its aspiring teacher-writers in ever-widening ripples.

A reaction was bound to set in at the same time that academe would perpetuate the bardic, "professional" tradition, for there was the Emersonian tradition lying fallow, capable of being picked up at any moment and hurled in the faces of the teaching post-Modernists. Besides, Whitman had early been identified as a model by, if not actually as the first of, the Modernists. The Emerson-Whitman tradition had been utilized in several ways by poets like Sandburg, Williams, Jeffers, and Pound. It was kept alive during the 1940's by such persistent if at first largely unheeded people as Charles Olson, guru of the anti-academic Black Mountain College; Kenneth Rexroth, uncle of the "Beats"; and solitary souls like Louis Zukofsky and Kenneth Patchen (who would, in the 1970's, be given credit as a progenitor of "concrete poetry").

As the 1950's dawned, so did still another generation of poets, most of them trained by Modernists and post-Modernists. It was a time for both stagnation and counter-reaction. In his introduction to the poetry section of *New World Writing 11*, Louis Simpson wrote, "The poets whose work is beginning to be seen—they are, most of them, under forty—have been called the silent generation. One critic finds them 'tame and fleecy'—that is, not wild and woolly. *Time* remarks that too many of the younger poets are 'wrapped in the cocoon of teaching.' Another critic complains of the 'elegance' of contemporary verse; it is a poetry of suburbia; the use of strict forms is interpreted to mean that the new poets want to conform, to make themselves tidy careers." Simpson went on to defend the younger poets as many others sought to defend them in periodicals such as *The Atlantic Monthly*, *The Saturday Review*, and the college quarterlies.

Why was it necessary to defend the young poets? What, particularly, was wrong with a whole generation of writers who were campus-oriented and workshop-nurtured? If all these defenses were necessary, it is obvious that there were in the 1950's many attacks against the poets of "the Silent Generation." That decade saw, in fact, the beginning of a massive reaction against formalist poetry which in the next decade turned into a rout. Many formalist poets themselves, including James Wright, Donald Hall, and even Simpson, turned against the bardic tradition, but for a while the defenses continued.

Rolfe Humphries, introducing *New Poems by American Poets*, observed that "the obscure and minatory seem to be disappearing." There was "considerable return to form." Although "W. H. Auden noted what he calls the beginning of a disturbing tendency for everybody to write alike," Humphries continued, this was not "necessarily a bad sign: everybody, more or less, wrote alike in the days of the Elizabethans, and in the age of Pope." (Neither of these statements is true, but all's fair in love and war, as the poet says.) For the most part these editors sought to protect these young poets who had had an audience for several years; who were, at the end of the decade, in their middle or early thirties; who had first books published by the Yale Series or the Wesleyan, Indiana, Minnesota, or Rutgers university presses; who had perhaps won the Lamont Award with a first book and who had established themselves in the faculties of various schools. But even the very youngest had their protectors.

In *New Campus Writing 2*, Nolan Miller and Judson Jerome wrote that "the younger poet is now principally concerned with forms and spare statement, rather than engaging himself with experiments in suggestion, allusion, and the tricky spangle of imagery." Finally Robert Frost, in his introduction to *The New Poets of England and America*, capped the defense with, "The poet and scholar have so much in common and live together so naturally that it is easy to make too much of a mystery about where they part company"—this from a poet who never finished college.

Sociologists attempted to explain the Silent Generation's migration to "the mainstream of English literature," to the campus, to the charcoal-gray mortarboard, as a search for security. Economists maintained—with the age of patronage of individual artists decidedly defunct, the age of bohemianism senescent, and the myth that commercial or antithetical careers are stifling to the artist becoming prevalent—that the campus was the only logical choice of livelihood for professional writers, especially poets who hadn't a prayer in the marketplace. To bolster this theory it was often pointed out that only Frost and Ogden Nash could make their livings from poetry; that there were not many like W. C. Williams, M.D., and insurance man Stevens.

But there were further explanations, perhaps simple ones, for the rise of the writers who worked in the academic house of mirrors. The Modernists had taken poetry about as far as it would conveniently go, and then some, in the direction of symbol, archetype, wit, and cerebration. When they were at their best they knew exactly where the limits of their art lay. At their worst they had a private language and a private continent where, ever since, literary sleuths have been tracking them. It became obvious that a limit had been reached. There was no longer reason for going on until that limit could be mapped out and, perhaps, further regions for experimentation and invention envisioned beyond its boundaries. Society grows, but its arts and sciences grow faster, if they are vital, and society must catch up before rapport is lost. If the head is separated from the torso, both die. In order for society to draw even, art must slow down periodically. This, it appears, is what happened in the 1950's. Almost without realizing it, the Silent Generation halted, looked rearward, and decided to retrench.

Or most did. A few of the "disaffiliated" decided to push on, like the "Beatniks," as the harbingers of the Psychedelic Generation were called in the Sputnik era by analogy (both were far out), for it turned out that the Beats were not an isolated phenomenon as many thought at the time. They were, instead, the advance contingent and prototype of a new wave of vatic poetry that was to spring in the 1960's from the biding dragon's teeth of Emerson and Whitman. Ginsberg, Kerouac, Ferlinghetti, Corso and company were the first myrmidons to arise from sparse soil. In San Francisco and Greenwich Village in the 1950's there could already be found in embryo all the elements of the activist Rappaccini's garden that gave American society the flower children of the 1960's. In the 1950's there were already LSD and a revival of the 1930's jazz weed marijuana.

But the major portion of the Silent Generation halted, looked around, and decided on a camping spot in the middle of the road. Everyone needs goals, new worlds to explore, however. The Silent Generation found theirs ready-made and made-to-order on the campus—in the classroom dedicated to the study of literature; in the periodicals, published on the campus, devoted to the extension and explication of literature; especially, they found it among themselves, the heirs of literature.

There are pitfalls to be noted and avoided, even on seemingly solid ground—the pitfalls of mediocrity, of imitation, of Alexandrianism, of innocuousness. In a society of poets there is a tendency to criticize one another's work and, in so doing, to make concessions that eventually lead to a formal or informal set of standards that are not necessarily of the highest quality. The danger in such a situation is that these standards may become so inflexible as to shut out influences, good or bad, that might induce poetic growth, a rise in stature if not an extension of literary boundaries.

Were such barriers to excellence erected in the 1950's, as the Beats and Black Mountaineers were claiming at the time? Broadly speaking, yes, they were. For instance, one of the unwritten laws was, "Show no sentiment." If one picks up an academic anthology of the period he will discover cleverness, urbanity, sophistication, wit, and a display of fine craftsmanship. If emotion was present it was often overcontrolled to the point where it became merely the cold image of feeling. A bit of sex was permissible, but not too much—perhaps a periphrastic description of the love act from which a moral was drawn. Humor was discouraged, but irony or even faint satire were all right. The offbeat or the outright whacky poem was proscribed. The only 1950's attempt to publish a humorous magazine of verse in this country, Richard Ashman's *A Huoyhnhnm's Scrapbook*, disappeared after a short but hilarious run.

At this point it might be interesting to note parenthetically that even the titles of the anthologies of the period were images of one another: *New Campus Writing, New World Writing, New Poets of England and America, New Poems by American Poets*. Even the Beats, who capitalized on everything in the grand Whitman tradition, titled their anthology *The New American Poetry* in reaction to *The New Poets* and thereby launched the so-called "War of the Anthologies" that carried into the 1960's.

Another rule was, "Do not stray from the iambic pentameter line." Of the first eleven poems in the first selection of *The New Poets* nine had first lines beginning with iambic pentameter; the other two were tetrameter. It took Robert Bly, on page twenty-three, to break the streak with his poem "Barnfire During Church." Certain poets, Bly being one, recognized the influence of the unofficial academy and attempted to do something about it. Bly's magazine, originally titled *The Fifties*, then *The Sixties*, finally *The Seventies* for one issue before its demise, attempted to counteract the academic influence but, in doing so, it merely set up its own set of antirules—"Use no classical allusions," for example. Nevertheless, it was Bly and his periodical that gave vent to the "pink cloud" that subsequently swallowed the workshops.

There were other rules and taboos, and the result was that many poets of the 1950's did not try to test the literary weather. They were polite, they were educated, their verse was competent though not always exciting. At the very least, however, the academic poets were professionals. They had dedicated their lives to writing poetry, and they made their livings in the same field, teaching literature.

Robert Francis in 1968 published a book titled *The Satirical Rogue on Poetry*. One of the items contained in it was titled "Professional Poet":

> Someone the other day called me professional poet to my face.
> "Don't call me that," I cried. "Don't call anybody that.
> As well talk about a professional friend."
> "Oh!" he said.
> "Or a professional lover."
> "Oh!"

Francis was himself at the time an academic of sorts; he had published in the standard places, including *New Poems by American Poets*, and his book *The Orb Weaver* had appeared from Wesleyan in 1960. This prose poem was clever and humorous, but something about it was troubling—there are, indeed, such things as "professional friends," people who are dedicated to helping others and who are paid for it. The world is full of them: Clergymen, nurses and doctors, firemen and policemen, Red Cross workers, Salvation Army members, and so on and on. What is wrong, then, with being a professional friend? Is a professional poet a whore or a gigolo? Clearly, by the end of the decade of the "Engaged Generation" Emersonian high-mindedness was alive and kicking in Amherst as in Haight-Ashbury.

In a materialist society it may be important to make the distinction between professional and amateur for the simple reason that any artist must take a basic step if he or she is ever to produce something extraordinary—one must transcend the snobbery of the bourgeois, the attitude that art is what everybody likes. One must overcome the mental set of what e. e. cummings called "most-people," that it is somehow undemocratic to aspire to excellence in anything except sports and movies; that it is fanatic to devote oneself completely to values so ephemeral and inutilitarian as to result in, perhaps, great poetry—"whatever that is," mostpeople might add.

If one of the major features of post-Modernism was the institutionalization of poets and poetry in academe, another was a similar establishment of criticism. For a while it even looked as though The New Criticism might take center stage and push literature to one side. Perhaps the only reason such a situation did not occur is that many of the Modernist and post-Modernist poets were themselves critics. In some, such as John Crowe Ransom, the critical component was often primary; Ransom stopped writing poetry for thirty years while he taught, wrote criticism, and edited *The Kenyon Review*. At last, in the 1960's, he returned to poetry— too late, unfortunately. His superannuated poetry was actually inept compared with his early classics such as "Bells for John Whiteside's Daughter," "Blue Girls," and "Captain Carpenter."

Perhaps one might automatically place Ransom in the category of professional poet. Certainly he was committed to poetry, but his commitment for those thirty years was of a different sort than that of a professional poet; he was dedicated rather to the idea of writing. That made him an agonist, the first important agonist of the bardic tradition in American letters if one excludes Stevens who was never an academic, though he was one of the academics' favorite poets.

In the post-Modernist period, then, the tenets of Modernism were institutionalized in the academy. For a brief period during the 1950's "professional" American poetry held sway and young poets were trained in the traditional techniques of poetry, aided and abetted by the New Critical "agonists" and theoreticians of professional poetry, in particular Cleanth Brooks and Robert Penn Warren, whose textbook *Understanding Poetry* was the Bible of the writing workshops. But professional poetry had developed its proponents late, a century after the "amateur" tradition had developed its major evangelist, Emerson, and its major prophet, Whitman.

When the 1960's dawned, the amateur line which, except briefly at Black Mountain College, had been lying fallow outside the Groves of Academe, reasserted itself, spurred by the Civil Rights Movement and protest against the war in Vietnam. Those poets who had been part of the Silent Generation suddenly became aware of the evils of the society that had bred them and began to react against formalism which, somehow, became equated with suppression and militarism, as the Rexroth quotation cited in an earlier chapter testifies. The academic poets were forced by their students, who were told not to trust anyone over thirty, to see professional poetry as being on the same plane with corporate, in- dustrial, and military professionalism. The professors became ac- tivists: the first "Poets for Peace" reading took place at University Circle in Cleveland in 1962, very early in the Illegal War. Poetry was henceforth to be judged, not in literary terms, but on its "sin- cerity." If the professor-poets didn't want to be exiled in their offices, they had better start being models of uncritical kindness. William Stafford began to emerge as an important teaching-poet.

Now the craft of poetry was jettisoned, and the art of language became unimportant while poet-teachers moved to raise the level of importance of protest, of conscience, of "truth," as Emerson had directed. How one said something was not as important as what one said, provided that what one said put the sayer on the side of the angels: Bly, who had for years been touting the wares of his friend James Dickey, fell out with him over a Dickey poem, "The Firebombing," from *Buckdancer's Choice* (1965). Self- examination was the rule of the day, but not self-criticism. Over- night a strange thing occurred: campuses full of professional poets were transformed into bastions of Emersonian doctrine, and they have not recovered yet. In the 1970's the Feminist Movement refueled the flickering fires of "The Movement." In the 1980's there are antinuclear fires smoldering just under the surface, and they break out every now and again. Nearly every fair-sized city still has its "underground" bookstore.

The result is that a whole generation of graduate poets has now gone forth steeped in the tradition of American anti-intellectualism. Pure of heart and innocent of craft, they flood the market with work that is largely vapid and "naked," in "open forms" that few dare to call gush. Yet if we look back on the activist anthologies of the 1960's—such volumes as the J.F.K. memorial anthology *Of Poetry and Power* (1964), *Poets for Peace: Poems from the Fast* (1967), and Denise Levertov's *Out of the War Shadow* (1968)—it is only too plain that most of the poems in them are painfully shrill and artless. The pitfalls into which the poets of the academic house of mirrors in the 1950's fell were shallow compared with the abysses of self-indulgence in which many of the same poets trapped themselves later on. The editor of the last anthology named stands as an example.

Denise Levertov's *Footprints* (1972) had to do largely with the war in Vietnam which raised many moral issues, one of the least of which, perhaps, had to do with the commitment of the antiwar "artist." It became obligatory during the war for artists of all kinds to comment, and take stands, on all sorts of things, not all of them clearly related. Some artists went far beyond symbolic gestures, to the point where they became famous for their activism rather than for their art—Whittier, Whitman, even Melville, are prototypes of this sort of American poet.

There is nothing wrong with this if one is a human being, but where does one draw the line, if one does, between activism and careerism? If one becomes famous for writing antiwar "poems," doesn't that person take as much guilt to heart as the manufacturer of napalm? Both profit from the war. One can be both poet and citizen. If the citizen takes part in acts of civil disobedience, that's one thing; if the poet writes verse after verse on the topic of war, gives readings of antiwar poems, publishes books full of such pieces, that's another.

Most of Levertov's antiwar poems in *Footprints* were embarrassing. They weren't art, they were harangue, or sentimental self-righteousness. The effect of such pieces was to draw attention to the poet as egopoetic sufferer for man's inhumanity to man. She was asking her readers not to pity the war-ravaged Vietnamese, but to pity Denise Levertov who hurt for the Vietnamese.

Levertov did not need her readers' pity—not for the war in Southeast Asia. The people caught in that war did. In her obsessive poems she asked her audience to focus on her words rather than on American actions, though it was action to which her words were meant to lead. The good poems in the volume were those that did not talk of war's evils in evangelical or pseudo-dramatic ways (in one poem the flakes of napalm delivered a sermon in monologue as they fell on the villagers).

What, then, is the state of post-Modernism as we approach the 1990's? It is in vast disarray if it is not in fact dead at last. Most of the attention granted to poets of the last twenty years has been granted to the amateur, and often the amateur of small talent at that. The professional poet is almost nonexistent at this juncture, and as for the agonist—no one ponders the question, What should poetry be in this brave new age? The New Criticism has gone to earth. "Structuralism," its successor, has gone to seed: one has no idea what the name was supposed to signify, for it had nothing to do with structure. It very rapidly evolved into a consideration, not of other genres of literature, but of Structuralist criticism itself—criticism as a branch of literature severed from literature, self-contemplative, hermetic. Already "Post-Structuralism" is feeding on the remains and Deconstructionism has been whelped. If the poets don't want to write poetry anymore one supposes the critics must have something to do, even if it is only to spawn new nonsystems and to contemplate their navels.

Sympathetic Magic

FORENOTE. There is some obligation on the part of the critic to let a reader know from what predilections, background and principles he speaks. This essay was commissioned by William Heyen for his anthology *American Poets in 1976*, published in the title year. It is unlike the other essays in *Visions and Revisions* because, to quote Heyen's Preface, his book "represents twenty-nine contemporaries writing on their own lives and work, on their art and on the people and landscapes that have entered their poems." If the Introduction is the prologue of this book, this essay is the epilogue.

I.

Several years back I was asked to write a comment on my work for a biographical dictionary. I said, "I regard myself as a formalist in the broadest sense of the word, not in the traditional sense, meaning perhaps an accentual-syllabic metrist; rather, in the experimental sense, meaning that the poem is the product of the whole poet, including his mind, bent on giving coherent language form to the human experience. I can only quote and echo the composer Benjamin Britten, who said, 'I try to write as Stravinsky has written and Picasso has painted. They were the men who freed music and painting from the tyranny of the purely personal.'"

I am a rather orderly minded person. I keep and file everything; my books are arranged alphabetically, grouped according to subject, and catalogued. However, my working surfaces are always cluttered and stacked with debris, except for brief periods when I attack the mounds and clear them away. During one of these frenzies recently I disinterred from my desk this note I had written to myself, or to the shadows of the cavern: "I see the poet as a *writer*. If he's got a philosophy, that's fine. But he ain't no priest, and he ain't no prophet, and he ain't no wild old man of the woods."

When I was eighteen and serving in the Navy, I made the conscious decision to attempt to become a poet. I sent a poem to the old *American Poetry Magazine*. I received a rejection from the editor, Starr Powers, that taught me my first great lessons. The poem, of course, was an egopoem, and Starr said, "I would eliminate the 'I do not know.' Readers do not care whether you know or not—they like to decide the answer for themselves, and arrive at their own conclusions."

She said, further, "All beginners write like this at first, and poetry, like all enterprises in life, goes through stages—this is one of them. Read more modern, emulate the eccentrics for a while, and finally you will emerge with a fresh, original style of your own." She recommended some books to me—a theoretical treatise, a practical book of exercises, some anthologies, all of which I bought and worked with in my spare time at the barracks. Shortly thereafter, she accepted for publication the first two poems I saw in print in a little magazine.

This all sounds so very rational, and one might begin to assume that I believe learning to write poetry is some sort of computer programming system. But I am the son of a minister who attempted to find God by seeking to understand himself. I am, further, an occasional anthropological kibitzer who was, and I am still, fascinated by Chapter XVI, "The Three Brains," in Arthur Koestler's book, *The Ghost in the Machine* (1968). Koestler quotes Dr. Paul D. MacLean's article, "New Findings . . . of the Brain," published in October 1962 in *The Journal of Nervous and Mental Disease*:

"Man finds himself in the predicament that nature has endowed him essentially with three brains which, despite great differences in structure, must function together and communicate with one another. The oldest of these three brains is basically reptilian. The second has been inherited from the lower mammals, and the third is a late mammalian development [the neocortex], which has made man peculiarly man. Speaking allegorically of these three brains within a brain, we might imagine that when the psychiatrist bids the patient to lie on the couch, he is asking him to stretch out alongside a horse and a crocodile."

That is, to me, an amazing and an illuminating passage. The science, I take it, is accurate—but so is the allegory, and it is this metaphorical language structure that provides the means for the flash of understanding. It is one of the essential methods of poetry. One may be *granted* insight, but one can *learn* to communicate it to others.

One of the prevalent post-Freudian tenets of certain kinds of latter-day Platonist poets is that the act of writing poetry ought to be an act of getting in touch with one's unconscious mind. Evidently these theorists believe that it is the lower brain—the crocodilian and horsey hypothalamus—that writes poetry, bypassing the specifically human "thinking cap" or neocortex. I have never trusted this theory. I consider that stories circulated about poetry-composing lizards and ponies are apocryphal. Koestler gave me some hope to believe that man is the only poet on earth:

To put it crudely; evolution has left a few screws loose between the neocortex and the hypothalamus. [In other words, there is poor communication between the "human" and the "animal-reptilian" brains. Furthermore, since the lower brain is incapable of conscious symbology, most of the "communication" seems to be upward rather than downward: It is unlikely that the thinking cap can directly get in touch with the brute.] The hypothesis that this form of schizo-physiology is built into our species could go a long way toward explaining the delusional streak in our history, the prevalence of passionately held irrational beliefs. . . .

Koestler's chapter is ostensibly about the physiology of the human brain, but it is in fact about poetry:

Man is a symbol-making animal; the proudest and most dangerous product of his symbol-making is language . . . its dangers are generally underestimated. In the first place, language is the main cohesive force within a given ethnic group, but, at the same time, it creates barriers and acts as a repellent force between groups.

I think I have always understood this. Therefore, I have always considered that poetry was not ultimately something private except perhaps during the process of composition. It is an act of reaching out to other human beings. Powers brought this home to me in her rejection letter. I have tried to keep it in mind ever since.

And I think I have always believed in the power of words that Koestler describes:

Without language there would be no poetry, but there could also be no wars.

The last pathogenic factor I shall mention is man's simultaneous discovery and rejection of death. The inevitability of death was the discovery by inductive inference, of that newly acquired thinking cap, the human cortex—but the old brain won't have any of it. Instinct and emotion passionately reject the abstract yet deadly idea of personal non-existence. This simultaneous acceptance and refusal of death reflects the deepest split in man's split mind; . . . you have to look at both sides of the medal: on one side, religious art, architecture and music in the cathedral; on the other, the paranoid delusions of eternal hellfire, the tortures of the living and the dead.

Poetry, then, for me, is a way of dealing with, and an expression of the whole of the human being. If it reflects us accurately, it will be both rational and irrational; it will be full of paradox, like ourselves; it is an exploration of the single self, but it is also a reaching out from the self to others like *ourselves*—there is ambiguity in this last word, for each individual has more than one self. Poetry is ambiguity made clear: the human being lying down beside the horse and the crocodile.

II.

Is a poet made or born? There is so much ground to cover here that I must begin by saying that I believe I may be a freak, but I hope not: I seem to have been born a formalist. There is a good chance that most young people who work in language are born formalists also, but they are unwilling to admit it, even to themselves, perhaps for romantic or irrational (if these terms are not in fact synonymous) reasons. It is a fact that much of my juvenilia was conscious experimentation in such things as accentual-syllabics, quantitative prosodies, alliterative accentuals, and so forth; it is also a fact that I had little or no notion such states and forms existed. It was not until I was in graduate school that I felt forced to admit my formalism. At that point it made no sense to deny what I was, and I began to study with a practical eye how poets wrote poems. Contrary to lore, I have found I was not damaged by knowing what I was doing. Much of my classroom time is spent in trying to convince students they will not find the creative candle snuffed out by applying intelligence to language. They may learn English language prosodies, or they may reinvent them, as I was doing young.

My students' trauma is the ordeal of unwilling recognition. They are afraid, like many adult poets, that if they once bring to the fore what they have done "instinctively," they will lose the instinct. But Koestler shows that poetry is not instinctive—it is a product of man's thinking mind. There is a difference between instinct and "second nature"—learning something so well that it comes easily and "naturally." I write very quickly. I seldom revise my poems much; nearly all the revision is done either while I am composing the first draft, or while I am typing up the second (usually final) version.* If I spend more than three hours on a poem, it is unusual.

My students find it hard to believe this fact when I tell them. It's true they feel they should be able to write quickly, but they usually discover that when they do it is flawed, or not totally realized as a poem. They have confused instinct with second nature; they have been using the English language all their lives, but they were not born knowing it. They learned their mother tongue by rote and by repetition and practice, but they do not remember; they thus assume that whatever they write ought to be poetry because the language seems to have come "naturally" to them. They fail to realize that the level of competence at which they have arrived has been achieved at the end of a long and arduous line of development. It is difficult for them to see that the poet must be many times more competent with language than the ordinary speaker, and that he or she must therefore continue this difficult developmental process. Understanding the elements of poetry and the capacities of the language will not damage their souls nor their talents. On the contrary, understanding will increase their capacities as the thinking cap grows more complex fold by fold. Thinking increases the ability to think, and imaginative creation is an aspect of thinking, not of primal emotions.

I do not argue that emotions have nothing to do with poetry— merely that poetry is a way of dealing with our emotions, our split minds, through language. In the dedicatory poem of *Awaken, Bells Falling* (1968), I think I managed to say what I believe poetry is:

> A Dedication
> *On a line by Joel Sloman*
>> If it is true that
>> "the sea worm is a decorated flute

---

* A typical manuscript page, of the title poem from *The Compleat Melancholick*, illustrates the profile article by Mary Doll in the *Yearbook 1984* of *The Dictionary of Literary Biography*.

that pipes in the most ancient mode"—
        and if it is true, too, that
the salt content of mammalian blood
    is exactly equivalent
to the salinity of the oceans
at the time life emerged onto the land;

        and if it is true
that man is the only mammal with a
    capacity for song, well, then,
        that explains why the baroque
worm swims in our veins, piping, and why
    we dance to his measure inch by
equivocal inch. And it explains why
this song, even as it explains nothing.

Poetry is for me, then, a product of the rational human mind attempting to deal with the reptile and the horse, the worm and the angels. Koestler's book means a great deal to me in terms of my understanding of the human condition. Something happened one summer after I read it that gave me the metaphor I needed to fix the concept of the three brains on paper where I could stare at them and watch them suck and claw: a family cat picked up a tick on its head. Our attempts to remove it were futile. Finally, my father-in-law simply broke off the tick's body and left the head imbedded in the cat's scalp. The situation kept turning over and over in my mind, until I recognized that I had taken both those minds into my own skull. The poem appeared in *The Weed Garden* in 1973:

Tick

    I am a cat with a tick
buried in my head. If I could speak,
    I would tell you I can feel
the insect head nestling within my

    brain, not just against the white
bone. I can sense its mechanical
    currents buzzing in the blood,
showing the mandibles how to clench,

the belly how to bloat, how
to make two lives one. It is not a
matter of will for either:
it feels my claws sliding in their sheaths;

I feel it growing stronger
on my substance.
My master?
As he looks at us, I see our two

minds sink into his eyes. We three
meet at the center of his thoughts. My
claws unsheath there. The insect
bloats in dark vessels. Here is where we

shall live together—a nest
of boxes, three separate designs,
three steps in Becoming, a
skull within a skull within a skull.

III.

Irrationality is as much a part of us as logical thinking—perhaps
more so in those of us who do not consciously make an effort to
control ourselves. There is no guarantee, however, that irrationality
will not break out in even the most rational individual. It is even
possible that irrationality controls the rational mind, directs it to
build logical constructs upon irrational bases—consider Nazism,
for instance, and its pseudoscientific rationale of the Superman, its
perversion of the theory of evolution. Those people who believe
that they are always in control, who deny the power of the uncon-
scious, are perhaps in most danger of succumbing to the reptile in
themselves. Perhaps there is good reason for our equating the rep-
tile with evil. But denying evil will not eliminate it; indeed, the
reptile loves to be ignored until it can rise to strike out of the
darkness where it lurks.

I believe, as I have said, that poetry is a way of *coping* with our
lower selves, *not* of getting in touch with the reptile in us, which is
impossible—our lower minds do not write our poetry. Nor does

science give us much help—at least to this point in our history—
with this coping. Poetry antedates science and the scientific sys-
tem, even as it is applied to the social sciences, but science has not
made poetry obsolete. It took many years before I was willing to
admit this, too: poetry is essentially religious in nature, even from
its sources. In all likelihood, poetry was first incantation and
prayer. "In the beginning was the Word, and the Word was with
God, and the Word was God" (John 1:1). That is one of the most
profound passages of the Bible.

Poetry was "invented" long before the present scientific system
of knowledge became the way in which Mankind understood its
world—obviously. The system that existed when poetry was new
is known today as the system of "sympathetic magic," and poetry
was very much at the center of man's way of knowing under that
system.

We as a race have lived under various systems of knowledge at
various times. Evidently, what has not been possible for us since
the development of the neocortex is that we should exist without
some sort of system. It should go without saying that our percep-
tions of reality have little to do with logic, even in the scientific
age.

What is "real" has to do with what we believe and experience,
not necessarily with what "is" in some abstract way. The reality
experienced by the madman is no less "real" for him than what is
experienced by the scientific observer. When the psychiatrist treats
the lunatic, two realities deal with one another, and six minds
interact; to extend MacLean's allegory, horse and crocodile,
man subjected, stare out of a cage at horse and crocodile, man
ascendant.

A system is a system, a way of ordering experience, and that way
of ordering controls our perceptions of reality; hence, we per-
ceived for thousands of years that Earth *was* the universe, and that
the stars were mere lights in the ceiling of the world. That system
stayed "true" until it was replaced with one that declared the Earth

to be the center of a much larger universe. The stars became the homes of gods wheeling about this earthly hub in constellations of bears and whales and dragons afloat in an ocean of darkness.

Then one sixteenth-century day a man named Copernicus happened along and threw humanity into chaos by pointing out that the Earth is merely one of many bodies wheeling about the sun, and the sun is the center of the universe. His system lasted only a little while, hardly long enough for the world to absorb, for in the seventeenth century Kepler and Galileo told the tribe that our sun is not the hub of creation, but merely an insignificant mote lost, with its planets, in a vast well of space—how vast and strange a well Einstein and his successors began to inform us in the twentieth century.

The system of sympathetic magic was based on two simple propositions: (1) The law of association: that which is once associated with something forever is associated with it, no matter what distances of time or space separate these things from one another. (2) The law of similarity: that which is like something, *is* that thing. Thus, if one could take a lock of someone's hair and weave it into a doll—a symbol of the person—then that doll *was* the person, according to both the laws of sympathetic magic, and one could stick pins, symbolic daggers, into the doll to kill the person. The clash of sympathetic magic with its replacement, science, in the seventeenth century, led to the Age of Witchcraft which culminated in the Salem witch trials of 1692, the worst outbreak of irrational societal madness until the Holocaust of the twentieth century.

Under the system of sympathetic magic one of the things that everything in the world had associated with it was its Secret Name. Every object, every person, every god had its Secret Name, and if one could discover the Secret Name of a thing, he might control it. Belief in the Secret Name was once universal. If we think hard, we can conjure up today various societies of the Secret Name that continue to exist in our culture—mankind evolves, adds to his lore, but little is truly lost. How many lodges and fraternities and sororities are there with their totems and rituals and secret names? Orthodox Jews still believe that the secret name of God must never be spoken, even if known, for that is the Word, the holiest of holies, and no mere mortal must ever believe the One God can be controlled, for this is to "take the name of the Lord in vain" hope of gaining one's desires. It is cursing. It is taboo.

It is also the basis for sorcery—conjuring of demons by pronouncing their secret names. There is magic in names, in conjure words, and this is the magic of poetry. Even if we do not believe in sympathetic magic, even if we no longer believe that the priest-poet controls the universe with the sorcery of runes, we can still believe that there is great power in words harnessed in the totally right way. If we cannot conjure gods and devils, we can, perhaps, conjure our deepest selves—our fears, hopes, beauties, uglinesses. And if the poet can do these things still, is he any different than he was in the beginning? For the system of sympathetic magic had at its core control and understanding of the way things are with Man and his realities—that much hasn't changed.

The new system of science attempts to deal with these things, too, but it is a rational method, and man is only partly a rational creature, as we have seen. That is why poetry is not necessarily a rational method: there must be ways to deal with our deeper selves, ways to handle our perceptions of reality that objective study just cannot manage. Some of these ways are poetry and music, philosophy, the arts. Alexander Pope said that the proper study of mankind is Man, and literature is no less a study of man than is science. In many ways poetry can go deeper into man than any of the sciences, for its roots tap something basic in our nature—this is true even on such a technical level as the sounds of the language.

There are theories that the rhythms of verse echo or counterpoint the beat of the human heart, and that the heart echoes the beat of the tides and waves against those primordial shores onto which our earliest ancestors climbed out of the sea-womb that gave them life. Some scientific evidence can even be conjured to support the point: "the salt content of mammalian blood / is exactly equivalent / to the salinity of the oceans / at the time life emerged onto the land"—perhaps the heart pushes blood as waves push water; perhaps language is the will of the blood made manifest. But poetry is more than sound and ritual. It is sensation and emotion, image and thought.

On the other hand, poetry should not be construed to be more than it is. Poetry can never be the original experience, the original vision of the writer, nor the essence of anything; it can only be the simulation of an experience or of a vision. Poetry is language art. If the poet is talented and knowing in the way of words, he or she can communicate a simulation, never the thing itself, to an audience. The poem can enter into the experience of the reader; it can be an experience in and of itself, but the poet cannot say the secret word and conjure a real demon.

This fact was borne in upon me one night several months after the death of my father in the fall of 1968. Like many people, I was a morbid person, afraid of death and not knowing how to cope with the fear. My father's passing greatly aggravated the condition. My conscious mind said, "Death is nothing," but my unconscious mind—sensing a threat, if Koestler is right—radiated terror. Since the lower brain knows nothing of symbolic communication, or words, my rational assurances to myself were of no effect.

My thinking cap, however, invented a situation that all of my selves could experience—not in "real" life, but in a dream. When I woke, I wrote the dream down. [This poem also appeared in *The Weed Garden*]. This is exactly what happened to me. It cannot happen to a reader in exactly the same way, but I can tell the story:

The Dream

 This is the story of a dream:
the gas station in a poor location,
 shadowed, even in daylight. The cars
  on their great tires—the 'twenties
or early 'thirties. But not many

 on the road. Perhaps evening is
coming on, darkness moving in, an air
 of something waiting in the gas pumps,
  behind the cooler. It is
summer. I am in attendance. If

 the lights were on perhaps someone
might turn off the road, drive up the old tar,
 ride over the sparse grass in the cracks,
  stop there, outside the dusty
window where I stand watching. Then with

 the thought, they are there—four of them
getting out of the square sedan. As they
 come filing toward the door, heads turned,
  looking at me through the hard
glass with their hard eyes, I know there is

 no way out. They'll find no money,
though—something in me grins at the thought, and
 the thought worries it. They are staring
  at me: the first is nearly
at the door. As our eyes lock I am

 shocked by the pistol in his hand,
by the flame in the muzzle, the shattered
 glass, by my blindness as the bullet
  enters the brain where I know
I am lost and reeling, blood pouring

 between my fingers, bathing my
eyes, and no sensation of pain, only—

  a vague regret that I will
now accomplish no more; certainty
 that this is death; amazement that
I can think with a shattered brain; knowledge

> that if I wake again they will
>   have saved me; rejection of
> the possibility. But beyond
>
>   these and above them: immense joy.
> It is over. It is nothing—nothing
>   I could have imagined. Mere joy, great
>   relief, release and silence.
> And I awake, but cannot believe
>
>   in waking. It has not happened,
> yet nothing more real has ever happened.
> Stumbling out of my blood into this
>   walking dream, nothing is left
>   except these words, images of weeds,
>
> dust, flame in a dark cylinder, and joy.

This poem may or may not affect a reader, depending on a number of variables. But the dream itself would have affected anyone—perhaps as it affected me, for my unconscious mind evidently believed the experience of its senses, that what waits at life's end is joy, not agony, for since that night I have not been nearly as morbid as I was formerly. I still am apprehensive about the process of dying, but I no longer lie awake at night in the chill hollow of the hand of darkness.

Poetry has its limitations. I wish my poem could do for every morbid person what the dream did for me. Though my poem may not be capable of giving relief from pain, perhaps it can provide hope, if I have learned how to write well enough in this language of ours, in this set of symbols our collective consciousness has invented in common—write well enough to convince the reader of this particular reality. Language is an imperfect substance, but the poet has chosen to try to build perfect communications out of it. It is an impossible task, but now and then one of us comes close.

IV

The more one knows about language, the more one can do with it. Powers told me to read—particularly the "eccentrics," by which I assume she meant the stylists and the experimenters. One can learn to write by reinventing literature in English, or one can read to discover what has been done and to visualize what still may be done. Both ways can work, but the latter is faster, less frustrating, more enjoyable and revealing: these are living voices from the past. Man has lived billions of lives. We may enter some of them if we have the imagination, and if we can read.

One day I was reading Robert Burton's *The Anatomy of Melancholy*, the great seventeenth-century compendium of knowledge on the subject we today call "depression." Burton, to drive home a point, mentioned "a silly country fellow" who "killed his ass for drinking of the moon, that he might restore the moon to the world." Two questions came to mind: was Burton right to scoff at the bumpkin, and why did the man commit such an act of violence upon the beast that helped him? Burton provided no further information.

I remembered the system of sympathetic magic and realized that this must have been an act of ritual sacrifice, not one of irrational slaughter. I put myself imaginatively into the mind of the countryman, attempted to perceive something of the system of reality in which he lived.[*]

The Moon of Melancholy

It was late when they came in
through the gate. He dismounted
beside the water trough, and the donkey
dropped its nose into the moon to drink.

He stood fatigued underneath
the wind scudding high cloud. No
light beyond reflection lit the windows
of the house. The barn soughed. The long grass

---

[*] The poem appeared in a book, the whole title of which is *The Compleat Melancholick, Being A Sequence of Found, Composite, and Composed Poems, based largely upon Robert Burton's The Anatomy of Melancholy.*

of the fields grew longer in
shadow laid over shadow.
The journey had taken forever. For
as long as it takes to remember,

he forgot where he had been,
and then recalled again. He
closed his eyes, listened to the beast drinking,
and was afraid, suspended

in that quiet of the mind.
When he looked again, when wind
had become too hollow against silence,
he found his eyes were opened,

but still he could not see. His
animal had drunk the moon
out of the water. He tried to discern
clouds, moon, sky, stars, the edge of the wind,

but found there a well into
which he felt himself to be
sinking. It was a vortex no world
could withstand. In the morning he wept

over the animal that
had carried him home; he wept
in the sun that had risen with him. He
remembered the image of

bone, restored as the blade sank
homing: The moon floating in
the trough of water and blood, and the wind
not quite too hollow to bear.

Burton had been wrong to scoff. He hadn't stopped to wonder at
human motives. He was writing a book about an irrational state of
mind, but for a moment, in haste perhaps, he failed to think about
the other person. He was too interested in proving his own point.

That returns us to Powers' main point in the rejection letter.
Though the poet must explore the self; though the act of writing is
done in solitude, if one forgets that one is merely one human being

among many, one is lost. If the poem the poet writes is merely private, it is nothing. It is miming in a mirror. One presumably already knows what one feels—need it be put into words? If so—if one does not know what one has to say until it is said—ought one to show the poem to others if those others are excluded from participation in the poem? Should the poet expect the reader to come to the poem simply because it has been written, or must the poet reach out and bring the reader in? Should neither care, or should both?

I believe that, at a minimum, the poet should care, both for his original experience, and for the reader, for what happens to one of us happens to us all, as in this final poem from *A Cage of Creatures* (1978):

Fetch

       To step out of a bedroom
      into a forest of darkness;
    to find oneself naked among brambles
and shagbark, a low wind making the flesh rise.
    To turn and discover there is no door,
       only bellbloom and shadow.

       And this is waking, the path
      beaten hard beneath heaven, stars
    among limbs bare of season. And between
the trees, glass—dark sheets parsing silence without
    image. In the wood only the mutter
       and crool of water wending.

       Pause and touch: merely surface
      smooth and cold among the boles. Search:
    only the ghost of reflection paling
under gaze. Walk, cover the ground. Know there is
    neither graith nor tackle to take the wood.
       Move as through one more tunnel.

       Stop when you feel him near. Strain
      to see who stands in the way, who
    holds out his hand, loof and hardel. It is
another mirror of the wood—no: likeness

of quicksilver. Behind him, a bedroom
lies rumpled in a gilt frame.

It is dark, but he is known.
He is the beast of whom they have
spoken so often in living rooms and
dreams. It is a familiar forest. This is
one's own path. It is the Fetch beckoning
welcome to the crystal glade.

Books Cited

Aiken, Conrad. *Collected Poems 1916–1970*. New York, 1970.

Allen, Donald M., ed. *The New American Poetry 1945–1960*. New York, 1960.

Baring-Gould, William S., and Baring-Gould, Ceil, eds. *The Annotated Mother Goose*. New York, 1962.

Berg, Stephen, and Mezey, Robert, eds. *Naked Poetry*. Indianapolis, 1969.

———. *New Naked Poetry*. Indianapolis, 1974.

Bodman, Manoah. *An Oration on Death*. Williamsburgh, 1817.

Bradstreet, Anne. *The Tenth Muse*. London, 1650.

———. *The Works*, ed. Jeannine Henley. Cambridge, 1967.

Brooks, Cleanth, and Warren, Robert Penn. *Understanding Poetry*. New York, 1950.

Browning, D. C., ed. *Everyman's Dictionary of Literary Biography*. London, 1962.

Bryant, William Cullen. *Poems*. Boston, 1821.

Burns, Robert, ed. *The Merry Muses of Caledonia*. Dumfries, 1801 and 1911.

Burton, Robert. *The Anatomy of Melancholy* (1621), ed. Floyd Dell and Paul Jordan-Smith. New York, 1927.

Campion, Thomas. *A Book of Ayres* (1601), and *Observations on the Art of English Poesie* (1602). Both to be found in *Campion's Works*, ed. Percival Vivian. Oxford, 1909 and 1966.

Carruth, Hayden, ed. *The Voice That Is Great within Us.* New York, 1970.

Davie, Donald. *Articulate Energy.* New York, 1958.

Dickey, James. *Babel to Byzantium.* New York, 1968.

———. *Buckdancer's Choice.* Middletown, 1965.

———. *Self-Interviews.* Garden City, 1970.

———. *The Suspect in Poetry.* Madison, MN, 1964.

Dickinson, Emily. *The Complete Poems,* ed. Thomas H. Johnson. Cambridge, 1955.

Eliot, T. S. *The Three Voices of Poetry.* New York, 1955.

———. *The Waste Land.* New York, 1922.

———. *The Waste Land: A Facsimile and Transcript of the Original Drafts Including the Annotations of Ezra Pound,* ed. Valerie Eliot. New York, 1971.

Francis, Robert. *The Orb Weaver.* Middletown, 1960.

———. *The Satirical Rogue on Poetry.* Amherst, 1968.

Gilbert, W. S., and Sullivan, Arthur. *The Complete Plays.* New York, 1938.

Gilder, Jeannette Leonard, ed. *Representative Poems of Living Poets American and English.* New York, 1886.

Hall, Donald; Pack, Robert; and Simpson, Louis, eds. *The New Poets of England and America.* New York, 1957.

Henderson, Stephen, ed. *Understanding the New Black Poetry.* New York, 1973.

Heyen, William, ed. *American Poets in 1976.* Indianapolis, 1976.

Hoffman, Daniel. *Poe Poe Poe Poe Poe Poe Poe.* New York, 1972.

Hough, Graham Goulden. *Reflections on a Literary Revolution.* Washington, 1960.

Humphries, Rolfe, ed. *New Poems by American Poets.* New York, 1953.

Jaynes, Julian. *The Origin of Consciousness in the Breakdown of the Bicameral Mind.* New York, 1977.

Kenner, Hugh. *The Invisible Poet: T. S. Eliot.* New York, 1959.

Koestler, Arthur. *The Ghost in the Machine.* New York, 1968.

Kreymborg, Alfred. *Our Singing Strength.* New York, 1929.

Leavis, F. R. *New Bearings in English Poetry.* London, 1932.

Levertov, Denise. *Footprints.* New York, 1972.

———, ed. *Out of the War Shadow.* New York, 1967.

Lewis, D. B. Wyndham, and Lee, Charles, eds. *The Stuffed Owl.* New York, 1962.

Library of Congress. *Proceedings of the National Poetry Festival 1962.* Washington, 1964.

Longfellow, Henry Wadsworth. *The Song of Hiawatha*. London, 1855.

Melville, Herman. *Clarel*. New York, 1876.

———. *Selected Poems*, ed. Robert Penn Warren. New York, 1970.

Milburn, W. H., ed. *The Royal Gallery of Poetry and Art*. Minneapolis, 1888.

Miller, Nolan, and Jerome, Judson, eds. *New Campus Writing 2*. New York, 1957.

Moore, Marianne. *The Complete Poems*. New York, 1967.

Nemerov, Howard. *Reflexions on Poetry and Poetics*. New Brunswick, 1972.

O'Hara, Frank. *The Collected Poems*, ed. Donald Allen. New York, 1971.

Omond, T. S. *English Metrists*. Oxford, 1921.

Pound, Ezra. *A Lume Spento and Other Early Poems*. New York, 1965.

Putnam, Eben. *The Putnam Lineage*. Salem, 1907.

[Puttenham, George]. *The Arte of English Poesie* (1589). Facsimile reprint, ed. Baxter Hathaway, Kent, 1970.

Richards, I. A. *The Principles of Literary Criticism*. New York, 1924.

Ross, Jean, ed. *The Dictionary of Literary Biography Yearbook: 1984*. Detroit, 1985.

Sargent, Epes, ed. *Harper's Cyclopedia of British and American Poetry*. New York, 1882.

Simpson, Louis, poetry ed. *New World Writing 11*. New York, 1958.

Smart, Christopher. *Poems*, ed. Robert Brittain. Princeton, 1950.

Sternlicht, Sanford. *The Teaching Writer*. Fort Smith, 1965.

Stevens, Wallace. *Harmonium*. New York, 1923.

Taylor, Edward. *The Poems*, ed. Donald E. Stanford. New Haven, 1960.

Thomas, Dylan. *The Poems*, ed. Daniel Jones. New York, 1971.

Tupper, Martin Farquhar. *Proverbial Philosophy*. London, 1838.

Turco, Lewis. *Awaken, Bells Falling: Poems 1959–1967*. Columbia, MO, 1968.

———. *The Book of Forms*. New York, 1968.

———. *A Cage of Creatures*. Potsdam, NY, 1978.

———. *The Compleat Melancholick*. Minneapolis, 1985.

———. *The Weed Garden*. Orangeburg, SC, 1973.

Turner, Alberta, ed. *Poets Teaching: The Creative Process*. New York, 1980.

Very, Jones. *Selected Poems*, ed. Nathan Lyons. New Brunswick, 1966.

Waggoner, Hyatt H. *American Poets from the Puritans to the Present*. Boston, 1968; rev. ed. Baton Rouge, 1984.

Weston, Jessie Laidlaw. *From Ritual to Romance*. Garden City, 1957.

Wheatley, Phillis. *Life and Works*, ed. G. Herbert Renfro. Washington, 1916.

———. *Poems on Various Subjects*. London, 1773.

Whitman, Walt. *The Complete Poems*, ed. Francis Murphy. Harmondsworth, 1975.

———. *Leaves of Grass*. Brooklyn, 1855, and subsequent eds.

———. *Selected Poems*, ed. Arthur Stedman. New York, 1892.

Whittier, John Greenleaf. *Justice and Expediency*. Boston, 1833.

———. *Songs of Labor*. Boston, 1850.

———. *Snow-Bound*. Boston, 1866.

Wrinn, Mary J. J. *The Hollow Reed*. New York, 1935.

Other Books of Historical Interest

Bell, Bernard W., ed. *Modern and Contemporary Afro-American Poetry.* Boston, 1972.

Bates, Charlotte Fisk, ed. *The Cambridge Book of Poetry and Song.* New York, 1882.

Bryant, William Cullen, ed. *A New Library of Poetry and Song*, in two vols. New York, 1877.

Carman, Bliss, ed. *The Oxford Book of Poetry and Song.* New York, 1927.

Court, Wesli. "Odds Bodkin's Strange Thrusts and Ravels," in *Poetry: An Introduction through Writing*, by Lewis Turco. Reston, VA, 1973.˙

Cullen, Countee, ed. *Caroling Dusk.* New York, 1927.

Dacey, Philip, and Jauss, David, eds. *Contemporary American Poetry in Traditional Forms.* New York, 1986.

[Duganne, Augustine J. H.]. *Parnassus in Pillory*, by "Motley Manners." New York, 1851.˙

Griswold, Rufus Wilmot, ed. *The Poets and Poetry of America.* Phila-1842.

Hughes, Langston, ed. *New Negro Poets U.S.A.* Bloomington, 1964.

Lowell, Amy. *A Critical Fable.* Boston, 1922.˙

Lowell, James Russell. *A Fable for Critics.* New York, 1848.˙

˙These four satires, taken in chronological order, form a satirical history of American poetry from the seventeenth century to the present.

Meserole, Harrison T., ed. *Seventeenth-Century American Poetry*. New York, 1967.

Monroe, Harriet, and Henderson, Alice Corbin, eds. *The New Poetry*. New York, 1923.

Perkins, David. *A History of Modern Poetry*. Cambridge, 1976.

Read, Thomas Buchanan, ed. *The Female Poets of America*. Philadelphia, 1867.

Rexroth, Kenneth. *American Poetry in the Twentieth Century*. New York, 1971.

Spender, Stephen. *Love-Hate Relations*. New York, 1974.

Stauffer, Donald Barlow. *A Short History of American Poetry*. New York, 1974.

Stedman, Edmund Clarence, ed. *Poets of America*. Boston, 1886.

Stepanchev, Stephen. *American Poetry Since 1945*. New York, 1965.

Untermeyer, Louis, ed. *Early American Poets*. New York, 1952.

Williams, Ellen. *Harriet Monroe and the Poetry Renaissance*. Urbana, 1977.

Index